Racial Prejudice

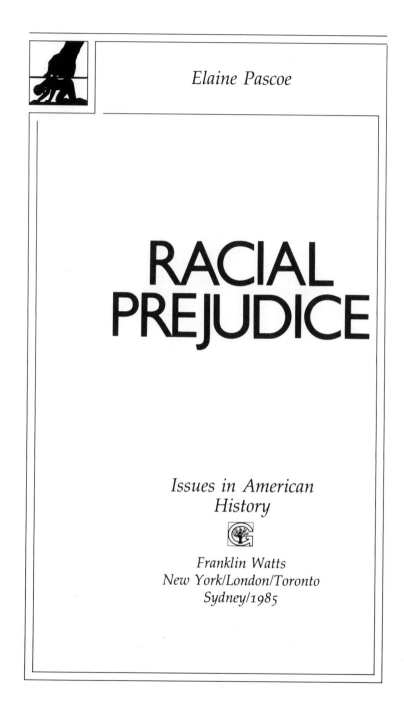

Elaine Pascoe

RACIAL PREJUDICE

*Issues in American
History*

*Franklin Watts
New York/London/Toronto
Sydney/1985*

Photographs courtesy of:
Bettmann Archive: pp. 20, 31, 72, 75;
UPI/Bettmann Newsphotos: pp. 41, 105;
Religious News Service: p. 43;
State Historical Society of Wisconsin: p. 57;
Museum of the American Indian,
Heye Foundation: pp. 59, 62;
Black Star: p. 67;
Library of Congress: pp. 76, 84, 97;
Fujihara/Monkmeyer Press, Inc.: p. 98;
George Zimbel/Monkmeyer Press, Inc.: p. 101.

Library of Congress Cataloging in Publication Data

Pascoe, Elaine.
Racial prejudice.

(Issues in American history)
Includes index.
Summary: Discusses the causes and history of
prejudice against minority groups in the United States,
reviewing the damaging effects of prejudice and
suggesting ways to eliminate it.
1. United States—Race relations—Juvenile literature.
2. Racism—United States—Juvenile literature.
3. Minorities—United States—Juvenile literature.
[1. Race relations. 2. Prejudices. 3. Minorities]
I. Title. II. Series.
E184.A1P34 1985   305.8'00973   85-8816
ISBN 0-531-10057-X

Contents

Racial Prejudice

For Carey

I | Equal—or Inferior?

> We hold these truths to be self-evident, that all men are created equal, that they are endowed by their Creator with certain unalienable Rights, that among these are Life, Liberty and the pursuit of Happiness.

Few people in the United States are not familiar with the above words. They are from the Declaration of Independence, written by Thomas Jefferson in 1776. Jefferson's statement, which marked the start of rebellion against Great Britain and led ultimately to the founding of a new country, summed up what many people believe is the single most important concept underlying life in the United States: Equality. The United States of America was to be a nation "with liberty and justice for all."

Yet few people know that Jefferson also wrote the following passage, in his *Notes on Virginia*, about black people:

> Comparing them by their faculties of memory, reason, and imagination, it appears to me, that in memory they are equal to the whites; in reason much inferior, as I think one could scarcely be found capable of tracing and comprehending the investigations of Euclid; and that in imagination they are dull, tasteless, and anomalous. . . . Some have been liberally educated, and all have lived in countries where the arts and sciences are cultivated. . . . But never yet could I

find a black that had uttered a thought above the level of plain narration; never see even an elementary trait of painting or sculpture.

Jefferson's meaning is clear—black people are less intelligent and less imaginative than whites and therefore clearly their inferiors. The blacks of his day, of course, were chiefly slaves, whose position in society prevented them from attaining any degree of education or accomplishment. Subsequent events have proved that, given the same opportunities, blacks and whites are equal in every respect. But the contradiction in Jefferson's writings—between the great founding concept of equality and the belief that the members of some races are inferior to whites—was shared by many people of his time. And despite all the evidence to the contrary, beliefs about racial inferiority persist to this day in the United States.

These beliefs persist because they are based not on facts and logic but on prejudice. The word *prejudice* comes from Latin words that mean "previous judgment." And a prejudice is just that—a preconceived opinion about someone or something; an opinion formed before its holder has gained the necessary knowledge or grounds for the opinion. If you are prejudiced toward something, you are predisposed to like it. If you are prejudiced against something, you automatically dislike it. If people say, "Blonds have more fun," or, "All lawyers are crooks," then they hold prejudices about blonds and lawyers—because there is no evidence to support either conclusion.

The reasons for prejudice are many and complex; some of them are explored in later chapters of this book. But for whatever reasons, at one time or another, groups of people in nearly every part of the world have developed prejudices against other groups that are different from them in some way. These prejudices have been based on nearly every factor imaginable—race, language, religion, social position, occupation, and so on.

Of all the forms of prejudice, however, racial prejudice is the most vicious and the most difficult to do away with. This is largely because racial differences consist of physical traits, such as skin color, that are obvious and easily recognized. You may be prejudiced against lawyers and yet pass twenty of them on the street—or even chat with some—without knowing their occupation. By the time you learn it, you may have already decided that the lawyers you met were nice people. This kind of experience tends to weaken prejudice. But people who look different are easily singled out. If you are prejudiced against them, you won't make the effort to find out what they're really like.

Prejudice thus becomes a roadblock to understanding. But it has more serious effects as well. The most common overt result of prejudice is discrimination—the "inferior" group receives unequal treatment. Discrimination can range from a social snub to denying members of the group jobs, decent housing, or an adequate education. At times prejudice can lead to violence, even to acts that are incomprehensible in the scope of their horror. During World War II, for example, the Nazi government of Germany executed approximately six million people on the simple grounds that they were Jews.

Prejudice in the United States has never reached the extremes that it reached in Nazi Germany. Yet, from the start, racial prejudice has been present, running like a countercurrent against the main flow of ideas and beliefs that have shaped the country. It has been directed not just against blacks but also against American Indians, Asians, and other racial groups. This book explores some of the underpinnings of racial prejudice in the United States and then examines how prejudices developed against different groups. The final chapter reviews the damaging effects of prejudice and takes a look at what might be done to wipe it out—and make the United States truly a nation of equals.

The Roots of Racism

Racial prejudice is not unique to modern times or to Western countries—its roots go back to ancient history in places scattered all over the globe. And prejudice did not spring to life suddenly in the United States. It developed partly as the result of attitudes that were widespread in Europe before the first British colonies in North America were founded. Some of these attitudes have been common to people at all times and in all places, while others were uniquely European. In the New World, certain circumstances and events worked to strengthen these attitudes until they were confirmed as full-fledged prejudices.

Ethnocentrism
Chinese texts from the third century B.C. describe with evident disgust a race of blond-haired, green-eyed barbarians that the Chinese thought were directly descended from monkeys. Another barbarian tribe was said to have sprung from a dog. Likewise, an old American Indian legend has it that both black and white races represent mistakes on the part of the Creator— the first man was baked too long and emerged black, while the second wasn't cooked long enough and came out white. On the third try, the Creator got the timing right and produced a golden Indian.

These ancient beliefs reflect an attitude that was crucial in the development of racial prejudice in the United States: Ethnocentrism. Ethnocentrism is the tendency of people to view everything around them in terms of the attitudes and values of their own group— their own way is always best. This attitude can be sparked by cultural differences such as language and religion, but physical differences tend to produce intense ethnocentrism. Thus, to the ancient Chinese, fair-haired tribes looked like monkeys or dogs, and to the Indians, whites and blacks seemed obviously to have been made incorrectly.

Although he had mixed feelings about slavery and in the end willed that his own slaves be freed after his death, ethnocentrism drew Jefferson to conclude that whites were innately more beautiful than other races because of their "flowing hair" and "more elegant symmetry of form." In fact, he simply found most beautiful that with which he was most familiar. An eighteenth-century student of racial differences, Johann Friedrich Blumenbach of Germany, summed up the problem this way: "If a toad could speak and were asked which was the loveliest creature on God's earth, it would say simpering, that modesty forbade it to give a real opinion on that point."

In the fifteenth century, European explorers began traveling to all parts of the world—to Africa, to Asia, and then to the newly discovered Americas. Their contacts with people of other races stirred up a hornet's nest of ethnocentric feelings. A case in point is this description of American Indians by Gonzalo Fernandez de Oviedo, an official chronicler of the Spanish conquest of the New World:

> [They are] naturallly lazy and vicious, melancholic, cowardly, and in general a lying, shiftless people. Their marriages are not a sacrament but a sacrilege. . . . Their chief desire is to eat, drink, worship heathen idols, and commit bestial obscenities. What could one expect from a people whose skulls are so thick and hard

the Spanish had to take care in fighting not to strike on the head lest their swords be blunted.

Thus, in true ethnocentric fashion, the Spanish assigned to an entire people qualities, such as cowardice and laziness, that can only be held by individuals. Unfamiliar customs were branded sacrileges and obscenities.

In a sense, this vehement reaction was surprising: The people of southern Europe—the Spanish, Portuguese, Italians—had had ample opportunity to become familiar with different races. Their lands lay near great trade routes leading to Africa and Asia. Even during the Middle Ages, when most Europeans had little contact with people from other parts of the world and believed that its corners were populated with monsters, traffic along these routes was heavy. Moors from North Africa conquered most of Spain in the 700s and continued to hold parts of it for the next seven hundred years. Yet time and repeated contact with other races had failed to dull Spanish ethnocentrism.

The experience of northern Europeans was different—until the sixteenth century, for example, the British had little contact with nonwhite racial groups. The first of the great British explorers, John Cabot (actually a Venetian who sailed under the British flag), reached North America in 1497–98. But it wasn't until the mid-1500s that British trading vessels began to travel great distances with any frequency. Then, as these traders came in contact with different racial groups, they reacted strongly.

When British trading ships began to visit the west coast of Africa, for example, one of the world's palest races came face to face with one of the darkest. The sight of the Africans—whose features, color, customs, and beliefs were so different from their own—stunned the British traders. Five West Africans who were taken to London in the 1550s to learn English so that they could then return to their homeland and help the traders caused a stir. Journals and reports of the time stress what the British found to be the ugliness of these people, their "disfigured" faces and their "black" skin. But no less disturbing were the language, customs, and beliefs of the Africans.

This shock at initial contact was repeated as British ships ventured farther afield—to the Western Hemisphere and to the Far East. By the 1600s, when the first British colonies in North America were founded, ethnocentrism was running high. And of all the factors that set the British apart from the races they encountered, color was the one that seemed to spark the greatest hatred.

The Concept of Color
To the English of the sixteenth century, color and physical appearance were fraught with meaning. It was widely held, for example, that a physical deformity was a reflection of some defect of the soul. Thus the villainous King Richard III of William Shakespeare's play was portrayed as a hunchback, although there was no evidence that the historical king was so deformed.

At the same time, the British attached great symbolic meanings to various colors. *Black* was a loaded word in English—in Elizabethan times as it is today. The *Oxford English Dictionary*, which traces the history of the language, notes that long before the 1500s *black* was used to mean "soiled" or "foul," "having dark or deadly purposes," "deadly," "wicked," "indicating disgrace," and so on. In short, black became the color of evil. *Yellow* has likewise become loaded with meaning—the color of stain, sin, and cowardice. *White,* on the other hand, connotes purity, virtue, beauty, and goodness.

Small wonder, then, that when the English of the sixteenth century were confronted with nonwhites, they concluded that the skin colors of these people reflected their characters. Ethnocentrism prevented them from believing that human beings had been created in any color but their own; the belief that outward appearance reflected the soul led them to speculate that darker-colored races were being punished for some sin. One popular explanation for the African complexion, for example, was that all blacks were descended from Ham, the son of Noah, who was cursed for the sin of disobedience. The curse is recounted in the Bible, in Genesis 9 and 10; the idea that dark skin might be part of the punishment was added by one George Best, an English adventurer of the late 1500s.

This wasn't the only explanation for color differences, of course. Best himself proposed that such differences might have stemmed from "some naturall infection of the first inhabitants of that country, and so all the whole progenie of them descended, are still polluted with the same blot of infection." Other writers argued that nonwhite races had been created separately (either before Adam and Eve or as an afterthought) or had descended directly from apes—theories that parallel in a startling way the Chinese and Indian beliefs about other races. And many people believed that color differences had environmental causes. A person whose skin was dark, for example, must have been burned by the sun. Indians were thought to redden their skin by rubbing it with grease and dyes.

Still, the association between skin color and character, coupled with the shock of seeing new and strange customs for the first time, led the British to conclude that nonwhites were defective and inferior. At a time when their thoughts were turning toward the establishment of an empire, this conclusion had important implications.

Colonialism and White Superiority

To the British, North America presented a rare opportunity. Portugal and Spain had already established empires—Portugal in Africa, Spain largely in Central and South America and reaching into the southern parts of North America. But most of North America was wide open, populated only by scattered Indian tribes. It was a fertile land, whose deep forests teemed with game and whose rivers and seas were filled with fish. And since the Spanish had found gold and silver in the New World, the possibility of unimaginable riches drew the British to North America like a magnet. Here, they thought, was a virgin land that they could claim as their own.

Establishing colonies in the New World was no simple feat, though, and one of the chief problems was how to deal with the native population. The Spanish solved this problem by conquering the Indian empires of South America, at first enslaving many of the Indians but ultimately intermarrying with them and blending them into their society. The British, on the other hand, simply displaced the Indians and kept them at arm's length. A second problem was the need for an ample—and cheap—supply of labor. In South America this was provided first by Indian and black slaves but later by a permanent underclass of peasants. In North America, particularly in the South, large-scale black slavery was the solution.

Why was the British approach different from the Spanish? One reason for the lack of intermarriage in

North America was that while many of the Spanish colonists were single men who eventually took Indian wives, the British colonists more often arrived with their families. But more important, many of the British colonists were religious dissidents who felt they were a chosen people, sent by God to cultivate the new land. For example, the Puritans of Massachusetts Bay Colony wrote in 1679 that "the Lord hath planted a vine, having cast out the heathen, prepared room for it and caused it to take root." Some forty years later, the New England preacher Cotton Mather wrote of blacks that "God . . . has brought them, and put them in your hands."

In short, the British colonists felt that it was God's intent that they rule over the other races. Many of the colonists felt it was their mission to convert these "heathen" groups to Christianity and to instruct them in the Western European customs that the colonists felt were so superior. Others looked with contempt on blacks and Indians as creatures of another species, unworthy of the benefits of Western civilization. In either case, the view that the colonists were God's elect—a chosen people—was a convenient one, since it justified the acquisition both of new land and of the labor required to till it. Thus, from the start, the concept of white superiority was firmly entrenched in America. In the late 1700s and early 1800s, religion slowly began to be less of a driving force in American society. But the colonists held onto the belief in white superiority—and they looked to science to justify it.

Anthropology and Social Thought
In the eighteenth century the early speculation on the causes of color differences gave way to more formal theories about race. One of the most widely held the-

ories was that different races had totally separate origins. The French philosopher Voltaire, for example, wrote that other races were as different from whites "as the breed of spaniels is from that of greyhounds"—not just in appearance but in intelligence as well. "If their understanding is not of a different nature from ours, it is at least greatly inferior," he wrote.

Two important ideas came together in the 1700s to give what appeared to be support to statements like Voltaire's. One was the system of classifying living things developed by the Swedish naturalist Carl Linnaeus. Linnaeus began his catalog of living things with primates, a category in which he included both apes and humans. He distinguished four human races, although he considered them to belong to the same species. In the late 1700s Johann Friedrich Blumenbach described five different racial groups and coined the term *Caucasian* to refer to whites. Like Linnaeus—and like most other scientists of his day—Blumenbach considered racial groups to be varieties of humankind. But some scientists took the concept further and held that races represented totally different species.

The second idea was the concept of the "great chain of being"—an idea that had been present since ancient times. In this view of the world, everything in creation stood at a specific rank, with inanimate objects at the bottom and humans at the top. There was an unbroken hierarchy—a chain from lowest to highest. This theory had always been somewhat incompatible with the Christian view of man as a unique being with an immortal soul. The gap between humans and animals seemed to break the continuity of the chain—until the new theories about racial classifications took hold. Thus, by 1800, people were advancing the idea that those in nonwhite races, particularly blacks, formed a link between whites at the top of the chain and animals below.

Scientists began to look for physical differences other than skin color to support this idea. Lengthy—and largely inconclusive—studies were made of skull size, shape, and capacity. Skulls were lined up in their supposed order in the hierarchy, from apes and orangutans through blacks and Orientals to whites. In 1799 Charles White, a British physician and surgeon, published a book called *An Account of the Regular Gradation in Man* that summed up these ideas. White contended that blacks were physically closer to apes than to whites and that, mentally, the "lower" races had "a power of thinking, but not profoundly."

In the view of eighteenth-century scientists, these different races had not developed in hierarchical order, one from another. They had been created separately and placed on the scale as they stood. This theory was, of course, an excellent defense for prejudice and discrimination—if a race was close to beasts on the scale, its members could fairly be treated like beasts.

The idea of separate creation was blown apart in the mid-1800s by the theories of evolution developed by Charles Darwin and Alfred Russel Wallace. They made it clear that all human races belonged to a single species—the similarities among them far outweighed the differences. But while the theory of evolution replaced the idea that races had been created separately as individual species, it did not alter the belief that some races were better than others. Other scientists quickly adapted the new ideas to bolster this belief—rather than standing on a lower rung in the great chain of being, nonwhite races were said to be less fully evolved than whites. They were still, in a sense, the links between whites and animals.

The search for racial differences went on, with scientists analyzing everything from the wrinkles in human brains to the chemical makeup of human hair. Various investigators divided people into as few as three and as many as sixty-three races. Yet to this day, the distinguishing characteristics of racial groups remain blurred. The range of physical differences within each group is huge, and many differences are caused by environment—climate, nutrition, and so on. Moreover, no one has ever succeeded in showing a direct relationship between a physical trait and personality or culture.

But lack of success in research did not stop the scientists of the 1800s from extending their theories. Gradually the concept of evolution spread from biology to society, to form the basis of Social Darwinism. This theory linked social development to racial characteristics, ultimately asserting that the concept of racial equality was absurd. "Primitive" (i.e., nonwhite) races were held to be incapable of developing the advanced social institutions of whites; to attempt to educate them was fruitless, as their minds were permanently childlike.

Thus science and social philosophy were used to support prejudices that had their roots in simple ethnocentrism. Of course, not everyone bought these theories—there were many people who spoke against them. But, meanwhile, other forces were at work bolstering prejudice in America, forces that still have this effect today.

Racism Intensified
Ethnocentrism and prejudice are reflected in all aspects of a society—from arts and literature to economic sta-

tus and government. Thus, when people look around them, they see these attitudes confirmed at every turn.

For example, as American literature developed, heroes were white as a matter of course. The heroines, who embodied the ideal of beauty, were milk-skinned and, more often than not, blond. Other races were portrayed as villains or provided comic interest—savage and deceitful Indians, servile blacks, Mexicans who snoozed all day under wide sombreros, scheming Chinese who chattered broken English, and so on. This basic format was kept alive not only in literature but later in film. Thus it became perfectly possible for someone who had never seen a black, an Indian, an Asian, or a Hispanic to hold deeply rooted prejudices against these groups, based on fictional representations.

Social scientists who have studied racial prejudice have found other factors that also tend to intensify it. One is the size of the minority group. The more members of the group there are, the stronger the prejudice tends to be. Thus prejudice against blacks has run strongest in the South, where great numbers of slaves were imported; prejudice against Asians, on the West Coast, where most Asian immigrants arrived; prejudice against Hispanics, in the Southwest and in other centers of Hispanic immigration. In each of these areas, racial prejudice has at times been whipped up by politicians who have played on white residents' fears in order to gain votes.

Prejudice also is strengthened when racial differences are compounded by differences in language, religion, and national origin. Such differences make the racial group seem all the more "strange" and threatening. And prejudice is stronger during hard times, because people are afraid of loosing their jobs and their economic status to those in the group below them. Thus they seize on anything in an effort to keep the minority group down.

Finally, as prejudice leads to racial discrimination, the results of discrimination tend to reinforce prejudice. Thus blacks who were denied education have been branded as stupid, and Indians who were restricted to barren reservations deemed lazy and unambitious. People who were prejudiced have seen their beliefs confirmed and have looked no further for the reasons, setting up a vicious circle of deprivation and disapproval.

The racial minorities in America started at the bottom of the social scale—the blacks as imported slaves; the Indians as a conquered people without rights; the Asians and Hispanics as immigrants to a strange land. We shall see in each case how prejudice formed against these groups, what factors worked to perpetuate it, and how each of the groups has worked to overcome it.

3 *Blacks in America*

Blacks form the largest racial minority in the United States and include people in every walk of life—statesmen, laborers, physicians, housewives, criminals, artists. Yet in the early years of this country, many whites formed a prejudicial stereotype of blacks, a standardized, negative picture that all blacks were supposed to fit. This stereotype has been proved wrong time and again, but it is still with us, subtly coloring people's attitudes even when they are not aware of it. Like the prejudice it reflects, it has been responsible for much of the discrimination blacks have faced.

According to the traditional stereotype, blacks have the following qualities:

- They are by nature a docile and servile people. They take orders well; in fact, they prefer taking orders to taking initiative. They lack the natural talent to be organizers.
- They are lazy. They will work only when absolutely necessary, and even then they will shirk, sleep on the job, and generally try to get away with doing as little as possible. On the whole, blacks would rather steal or live on welfare than hold a job.
- They are less intelligent than whites. They have difficulty with anything but the most basic tasks, and even then they are apt to break or mislay their tools.
- They have no sense of moderation or of good management. If they get a little money, they will gamble it away or spend it on gaudy clothes or a flashy car. They will party all night even though they have to be at work at six the next morning.

- They are physically stronger than whites and have stronger sexual instincts. All black men prefer white women to women of their own race.
- Blacks form family ties loosely, at best. Fathers routinely desert their wives and children.
- They are an emotional people. Emotions such as love and hate govern all their actions; they are rarely controlled by intellect. At the best, this means that blacks are like children. At the worst, it means that beneath the skin of every black person lurks a murderous beast that may spring without warning at any time.

Like all stereotypes, this picture takes a few individual characteristics and projects them onto an entire group. No group of people, of course, could exhibit all of these qualities universally; single individuals of any group might have some of them. Closer analysis shows this stereotype to be even more ridiculous than most because it contains such blatant contradictions. For example, blacks are supposed to be naturally lazy but at the same time have the energy to party all night. They are emotional and yet form loose ties. They are said to be docile children on the one hand and murderous beasts on the other.

The fallacies and contradictions can be explained by looking at how the stereotype formed. Some of its elements reflect whites' irrational fears of a group that looks different from them. Others are simply newer versions of arguments that were first advanced in defense of slavery.

Blacks as Slaves

Slavery as an institution is probably as old as humankind. Certainly it was common in the ancient world, among the Egyptians, Greeks, and Romans. But the slavery that developed in America was unique in that it was racial slavery. In ancient Greece, for example, a person of any race might through conquest or misfortune become a slave. But in North America, only blacks were enslaved, never whites.

In fact, racial prejudice and the practice of holding black workers for life preceded formal, legalized slavery in the New World. The first blacks to be taken to North America arrived in Jamestown, Virginia, in 1619—not as slaves but as indentured servants. Indentures (the agreements under which these servants worked) were the usual means of obtaining cheap labor in the British colonies; servants worked a set number of years and then were free to return home or make their own way in the New World. This was the pattern followed by many Irish and other people who emigrated to America in colonial times. But for blacks the pattern changed: Their servitude became perpetual and was passed on to their children. There were several reasons.

First, the British had before them the example of other nations, which had been enslaving blacks for some years. Slavery was common among Africans themselves. If two groups fought, the victors often took the losers captive and held them as slaves. But by the eighth century, African slaves were already being exported in quantity by the Arabs, who had conquered North Africa. Arab slave traders traveled into the center of the continent to buy or capture slaves, and these slave traders became notorious for their cruelty. Countless blacks died on the long trip north across the Sahara.

A number of these slaves were sold in Spain and Portugal, and by the end of the fifteenth century these countries were sending raiding parties of their own to capture African slaves. As Spain's empire in the New

World began to take shape, more and more African slaves were sent there. The British were fully aware of the practice; in fact, some British merchants were involved in the profitable Spanish slave trade. By the early 1600s the practice had been picked up in Britain's West Indies colonies. From there it traveled to New England, which traded heavily in the islands.

But the concept of racial slavery wasn't simply borrowed from the Spanish. The British and the Spanish were enemies and competitors in the New World, and the British had no love or admiration for Spanish institutions. In fact, stories of the Spaniards' mistreatment of slaves regularly circulated as evidence of their cruelty and inhumanity. The English as a rule held slavery to be an evil, something that ran counter to the natural dignity of man.

Racial slavery became an accepted practice in North America for two quite different reasons: It filled a need, and it fit with certain preconceived notions that the white settlers there already had about blacks. This was, as we have seen, an era of extreme ethnocentrism, when the English felt they were by nature superior to other races—perhaps even set above them by God.

The Puritans of New England, for example, had strong but strangely clannish views about personal freedom—a Puritan law of 1641 stated that "there shall never be any bond-slavery, villenage or captivitie amongst us; unlesse it be lawfull captives taken in just warrs, and such strangers who willingly sell themselves, or are solde to us." The fact that blacks were considered strangers was borne out by other aspects of

Slaves being brought ashore
at colonial Jamestown

New England life—blacks were not allowed to train for the Massachusetts militia, for example. The Puritans apparently took the ethocentric view that these people, who looked so different, must be a menace to society.

New England's climate and geography dictated that it would become a region of small farms. It needed few slaves in comparison to the colonies around the Chesapeake Bay and to the south, where large plantations were springing up to grow tobacco and other crops. These colonies had difficulty attracting indentured servants from England and other European countries to perform the backbreaking field work required on the plantations. But there was no need to attract blacks—they could simply be imported. Thus it was in the South that slavery took hold most deeply. And here, again, racial prejudice went hand in hand with the practice.

Slavery developed gradually in the South, and exactly when it took root is unclear. In Virginia during the 1640s, for example, blacks were already being treated differently from whites. Blacks were often listed in early census reports simply as a number of "Negroes," without names. They were not permitted to keep or bear arms. Romantic unions between blacks and whites were severely punished. The number of black servants who were bonded for life in Virginia at this time is not known, but it is certain that black servants served far longer terms than the three to seven years customary for white servants. Black women as well as men were considered suitable field workers, although white women were not.

It is clear that by 1660 large numbers of blacks were being held as slaves for life, with their children to be held after them. There is no evidence that any white servant was ever held in this manner. In 1662 Virginia adopted the first law recognizing that some blacks were to be perpetual slaves. Maryland followed suit two years later with a statute proclaiming, "All Negroes and other slaves shall serve Durante Vita [for life]."

Thus prejudice and slavery were linked from the beginning in America. By 1700 black slavery was an accepted practice throughout the British colonies. The pace of the slave trade picked up dramatically, and by 1800 there were more than 800,000 slaves in Maryland, Virginia, the Carolinas, and Georgia. The conditions under which they lived not only ensured that they would remain at the bottom of society but also gave rise to many elements of the prejudicial stereotype of blacks.

Slavery and the Stereotype
The slaveholders of North America didn't use guards, chains, or fences to prevent escape. Instead, they relied on psychology. They kept their slaves totally dependent on them and, at the same time, ignorant of the outside world and fearful of punishment.

The slaves' food, clothing, and housing came entirely from their masters. On the whole, most North American slaves weren't mistreated—at least in comparison to the treatment received by slaves in the Spanish colonies, who often died from overwork. North American slave owners looked on their slaves as investments, and they wanted their slaves to live. But by today's standards, conditions were appalling—the food was poor and the housing primitive.

Worse, the slaves had absolutely no hope of improving their lot. Slaves were not allowed to amass property of their own. If they escaped, there was literally nowhere to go. Recapture was inevitable, and the result would most likely be a beating or sale into some even harder way of life. Even if they managed to evade recapture, there was no way for them to earn a living.

Most slaves were intentionally taught to do field work but nothing else—in fact, in most of the South it was a crime to teach a slave to read or write, although some house slaves managed to pick up some education.

Given these conditions, it is not surprising that most slaves did as they were told without objecting. It's also not surprising that few slaves were inclined to do more work than was necessary to avoid a beating, or that they occasionally stole food or other necessities that they could not buy. Yet, rather than recognizing the injustices of the slaveholding system, slave owners seized on these practices as proof that blacks were not the equals of whites. The rare blacks who overcame the odds—Benjamin Banneker, the mathematician, and Phyllis Wheatley, the poet, for example—were dismissed as oddities.

Similarly, because they wanted the absolute loyalty of their slaves and also because they wanted the freedom to sell individual slaves at any time, plantation owners generally discouraged strong family ties among slaves. Slaves were not permitted to use surnames, their marriages had no legal status, and on some plantations they could be punished for referring to family members as "my mother" or "my brother." Despite this, most slaves formed strong family bonds, joining in lifetime marriages and often passing down for generations "underground" surnames that whites never heard. Yet the external picture of weak ties, which had been imposed by whites, was then taken as evidence of a lack of values on the part of blacks.

By the 1800s the stereotypical picture of blacks had begun to emerge—docile, ignorant, lazy, dishonest, lacking strong values. It had been created by the prejudice that placed blacks in the position of slaves. But now prejudice was bolstered by the stereotype, and slavery found justification in it.

The Split Between North and South
Supporters of slavery had need of justification—debate on the institution was growing intense. The ideals of equality voiced during the American Revolution had made many people think twice about keeping others in bondage. Thus, in 1808, the importation of new slaves was banned. By this time most Southern states had begun passing laws to improve conditions for the slaves. And most Northern states had begun to announce that in the future, slavery would be banned. The effect of these pronouncements was that Northern slaves were sold in the South, so slavery became a regional problem. By 1860 there were about four million slaves in the South.

Opposition to slavery was strongest in the North, and there a romanticized picture of blacks developed. But the abolitionists, as the opponents of slavery were called, did not go so far as to suggest that blacks were the equals of whites—on the contrary, many of their arguments were based on the injustice of a supposedly superior race taking advantage of an inferior one. The abolitionist image of blacks drew heavily on popular novels of the 1820s and 1830s that presented slaves as "good darkies"—people who were, in the words of one Northern preacher of the time, "singularly childlike, affectionate, docile, and patient." The best-known example of this viewpoint is Harriet Beecher Stowe's novel *Uncle Tom's Cabin* (1852), in which the black characters exude meekness, simplicity, and childlike faith.

In the South, meanwhile, a more negative picture of blacks was emerging. The late 1700s saw a number of bloody slave revolts in the Caribbean, and this raised fears among slave owners. In 1831 a slave uprising broke out in Virginia, led by Nat Turner. Sixty whites were killed. These events introduced a new element into the black stereotype—the black as "murderous beast." Blacks were seen as savages who had been "domesticated" by slavery; loosen the bonds, and they would revert to their previous state. As one proslavery writer put it, "The madness which a sudden freedom from restraint begets—the overpowering burst of a long buried passion, the wild frenzy of revenge, and the savage lust for blood, all unite to give the warfare of liberated slaves, traits of cruelty and crime which nothing earthly can equal."

The element of fear, coupled with the South's dependence on slave labor, served to make most Southerners more staunchly proslavery than ever. Interestingly, much of the fear was directed not against slaves but against free blacks, of whom there were nearly five hundred thousand in 1860. Southern states tightened their "black codes," the laws that regulated the lives of both slaves and free blacks. They also began to censor abolitionist literature and even screened the mails.

The North-South split on slavery was, of course, one of the central issues leading up to the Civil War. But the concept of blacks as equals in an integrated society was never part of the Northern cause. Many abolitionists believed that once freed, blacks would want to return to Africa or at least would leave the United States. Abraham Lincoln (who was not an abolitionist) advocated this course as the only way to reconcile the "self-interest" and "moral sense" of the whites. In an 1858 debate with Stephen O. Douglas, he clearly stated his opposition to an integrated society—and displayed considerable prejudice of his own:

I am not nor ever have been in favor of bringing
about in any way the social and political equality of the white and black races . . . I am not
nor ever have been in favor of making voters or
jurors of negroes, nor of qualifying them to hold
office, nor to intermarry with white people; and
I will say in addition to this that there is a physical difference between the white and black races
which I believe will for ever forbid the two races
living together on terms of social and political
equality. And inasmuch as they cannot so live,
while they do remain together there must be the
position of superior and inferior, and I as much
as any other man am in favor of having the superior position assigned to the white race.

Lincoln did oppose the spread of slavery to the United
States' frontier territories, however, because he felt
slavery was morally wrong. Largely as a result of this
position the Southern states began seceding promptly
on his election in 1860. During the early years of the
Civil War, Lincoln resisted pressure to free the slaves,
largely because he needed the support of slave owners
in states such as Missouri that had not seceded. Finally, in 1863, he issued the Emancipation Proclama-
tion, which freed slaves in the South. It was followed
three years later, after the end of the war, by the Thir-
teenth Amendment to the Constitution, which prohibited slavery forever.

The end of the war in 1865 found the United States
faced with a difficult problem—what to do with several
million blacks who were poor to the point of destitu-
tion and essentially had no place in society. The Freed-
men's Bureau, a federal agency that operated from 1865
to 1872, attempted to help them, with only limited suc-

cess. The idea of shipping former slaves to new homes in Africa or elsewhere was gradually given up as impractical. It appeared that blacks were in the United States to stay—but in what position?

Reconstruction

The Southern view was clear: Blacks might have been freed, but that did not mean that they should be voters or enjoy full rights as citizens. Immediately after the war Southern states adopted new "black codes" that gave prejudice the force of law. South Carolina's code of 1866, for example, stated that the races were "separate and distinct, the one the highest and noblest type of humanity, the other the lowest and most degraded"; to give blacks full rights would be "treason to race." Most of the codes barred blacks from voting, serving on juries or in the military, holding office, testifying in court against whites, and assembling without a permit. They were required to have passes to move from place to place and could be fined for not working.

The Northern answer was the Reconstruction Act of 1867, which in effect placed the South under military rule and forced Southern states to approve the Fourteenth Amendment, which guaranteed equality under the law. Blacks registered to vote with soldiers standing at the polls. Meanwhile, the political rights of whites who had supported the Confederacy were sharply restricted. As a result, political control fell mostly to Northern opportunists (carpetbaggers) and blacks.

Many of these people were inexperienced in government—slavery had hardly prepared blacks to be officeholders. Others took advantage of the situation and abused their powers; bribery and corruption were common. The result was that racial prejudice was hardened. Many Southerners claimed to see their worst fears realized in the years after the war, and they pointed to the Reconstruction governments as evidence that blacks were unfit to exercise political power. With no political power of their own, they began forming vigilante groups such as the Ku Klux Klan to intimidate the blacks.

Gradually the Northern attitude softened, and the Southern whites regained their political rights. In state after state, local white governments took back control. The last federal troops left the South in 1877. But bitterness remained, and the stage was set for one of the most intense periods of racial prejudice in the nation's history.

The South in the Late 1800s

The prejudicial stereotype of blacks survived the Civil War and Reconstruction to emerge full-grown in the late 1800s. As it had before the war, it took two forms. Some Southern whites took a paternalistic view of blacks— they were like children who should be guided to their proper place in society. One of the leading supporters of this view was Joel Chandler Harris, an editor of the *Atlanta Constitution*, who wrote the Uncle Remus stories around 1880.

In some of the stories, Uncle Remus is a typical plantation "good darky" who spins tales for children. In others, he strolls through Atlanta observing the postwar condition of blacks and making comments such as, "You slap de law onter a nigger a time or two, an' larn 'im dat he's got fer to look atter his own rashuns an' keep out'n udder foke's chick'n coops, an' sorter coax 'im ter feed 'is own chilluns, an' I be blessed ef you ain't got 'm on risin' ground!" Rising—but not equal. Paternalistic whites urged others not to worry that the black would rise above them. "That," explained another writer, "cannot be done unless you get below him."

A second, harsher view saw blacks as a menace to society. If blacks weren't kept in an inferior position, the people who took this view warned, the result would be race war or "contamination" by racial mixture. This view relied heavily on the anthropological theories of the day—theories that saw the white race as superior and racial conflict as inevitable. It also played heavily on fear, presenting blacks chiefly as potential criminals and rapists who lusted after white women. It was the logical successor to the prewar fear that only slavery controlled the "beast" in the black person's soul.

This view gained ground during the 1880s for several reasons. One was a slide in the Southern economy, for which blacks made convenient scapegoats. Another was that since the war, blacks and whites had lived more and more separately. Few whites spoke with blacks or knew how they lived or what they thought; therefore they became more and more suspicious of blacks. By 1890 the harsher view had largely overruled the more moderate one.

The result was discrimination. The Southern states passed "Jim Crow" laws that stripped blacks of their rights. Poll taxes (fixed fees charged to each voter) and difficult literacy tests were used to deny them the vote; "grandfather clauses" in state laws waived these re-

Prejudice against blacks intensified during the Reconstruction era in the South, and lynchings and other terrorists acts by so-called vigilante groups were common practice.

quirements for those descended from people who had voted before 1867—who, of course, were white. Blacks were forbidden access to schools and other facilities that served whites. Instead, they were offered "separate but equal" facilities—facilities that were indeed always separate but seldom equal.

At the same time, one-sided race riots and lynchings took their toll of black lives. At the turn of the century, blacks were being lynched at the rate of one hundred a year. Enterprising politicians even campaigned on the issue, asserting the public's right to take these steps. As one Georgia politician described it, whites had to "lynch [the black] occasionally, and flog him, now and then, to keep him from blaspheming the Almighty by his conduct, on account of his smell and his color."

The moderate view did not die out. For example, Southern moderates were strong supporters of Tuskegee Institute, the school founded by Booker T. Washington to teach blacks industrial and other practical skills. Moderate whites felt that such education was appropriate and would help blacks find their proper place in society.

But for the time being, this remained the minority view. And in the rest of the country, people largely closed their eyes to the increasing racial hatred in the South. In 1896 the United States Supreme Court ruled that the "separate but equal" concept was constitutional. Many Northerners felt they had learned a lesson from the difficulties of the Reconstruction era, and they were no longer willing to fight for blacks' rights— as a 1900 editorial in *The New York Times* remarked, "[Northerners] no longer denounce the suppression of the Negro vote in the South as it used to be denounced in the reconstruction days. The necessity of it under the supreme law of self-preservation is recognized."

Besides, by the turn of the century, Northerners could no longer claim that race problems existed only in the South.

The Movement North

Since before the Civil War, a number of blacks had steadily made their way from the agricultural, slave-holding states of the South to the industrial cities of the North. The northward flow increased somewhat in the years just after the war and then, in the late 1800s, jumped dramatically. Twice as many blacks moved to the North and the Midwest in the 1890s as had done so in the 1880s. By 1920 the number had doubled again, and it did so once more in the 1920s. In the ten years between 1920 and 1930, more than 750,000 blacks left the South. In all, the migration of blacks from South to North rivaled the great waves of immigration from abroad that the United States also saw at this time.

The increase in Southern racial prejudice at the turn of the century was an important reason for this great migration, but it was not the only reason. Southern cotton crops had been attacked by the boll weevil, so there was less work for blacks on Southern farms and plantations. At the same time, the industries of the North were expanding, offering new opportunities. During World War I, immigration from Europe halted— just at the time that factories needed more workers to churn out arms. Most of the blacks who headed north, then, were job seekers, young or in the prime of life. They saw the North as a land of opportunity.

Most of the blacks who had lived in the North before this great influx were moderately successful working-class people—skilled laborers, craftsmen, waiters, and so on. They were often better off than recently arrived immigrants from Europe. And while some Northern communities attempted to segregate blacks and whites, by and large, segregation had not taken hold. Neighborhoods in the large industrial cities tended to be integrated. Northern blacks could vote and were occasionally elected to public office, and they mixed with whites socially and in business.

The large-scale migration of blacks changed this situation. The new arrivals, who were mostly unskilled and uneducated, were at first resented by Northern blacks and whites alike. But whites soon allowed their resentment to spill over to include all blacks. Neighborhoods became segregated, and black ghettos formed in the major cities. Blacks who attempted to move into white neighborhoods were dealt with sharply—chapters of the Ku Klux Klan appeared in the North, and some cities adopted laws that legalized residential segregation. As the numbers of blacks increased, so did the barriers to their success. Blacks were barred from certain jobs and schools and from white society generally.

Thus Northern blacks found themselves increasingly cut off from the opportunities they had sought. Poverty, frustration, and lack of education were features of ghetto life, and they contributed to high rates of crime and disease. Just as many Southerners had found justification for their prejudice in the social conditions under which blacks lived, many Northerners pointed to crime and disease in black neighborhoods as evidence of racial inferiority.

But the extreme racial hatred that marked the South at this time never took hold in the North. Most Northerners took the moderate line, holding that blacks were "children" who could be educated to fit into society.

Like Southern moderates, they supported educational programs such as that at Tuskegee Institute.

The Depression of the 1930s temporarily halted black migration to the North—jobs were not to be had anywhere. Thus the eve of World War II found blacks frozen as a subclass in American society. Scientists and sociologists continued to support theories that blamed racial characteristics for the blacks' problems, and few people spoke out against the social injustices that were the true causes. Prejudice against blacks seemed to be an integral part of American society, too firmly rooted ever to be weeded out.

4

Blacks in a Time of Change

The past fifty years have seen enormous changes in the position black people hold in American society. The laws that forced blacks to accept low-quality housing, education, and jobs have been stricken from the books. Blacks are no longer required to eat at separate restaurants or take the back seats in buses, as they once were in the South.

Yet to a large extent, blacks remain second-class citizens. In some areas the lines separating blacks and whites are as clearly drawn as ever, even if these lines no longer have the force of law. Legalized discrimination may be a thing of the past, but the underlying racial prejudice that sparked discrimination in the first place seems to linger on.

The fight for full equality has seesawed back and forth, with gains followed by setbacks that are in turn followed by new gains. All the same, blacks in the United States are closer to true equality today than at any point in history. The barriers that kept them back began to fall in the 1930s, and they are still being broken down.

New Ideas, New Opportunities

By the late 1930s several factors had combined to put racial prejudice in a new perspective in the United States. One was a change in the attitudes of blacks themselves.

The great migrations north and the creation of ghettos in the cities had served to make blacks more aware of their race. As the black communities in the cities became increasingly sophisticated, this new racial consciousness was reflected in several ways. One was a cultural movement known as the Harlem Renaissance, or the New Negro Movement. Black writers such as Langston Hughes and James Weldon Johnson spearheaded the movement, expressing the thoughts and feelings of the emerging black community.

Blacks had also become increasingly aware of—and frustrated by—the discrimination they faced. Organizations such as the Urban League and the National Association for the Advancement of Colored People (NAACP) had begun to form before World War I to try to improve conditions for blacks. These organizations had little success at first. The NAACP, for example, managed to bring an antilynching bill before Congress in 1921, but Southern senators blocked the bill and it never came to a vote. But the new black organizations served as voices for the black community, speaking out on black problems and bringing them to the attention of whites.

The years following World War I also saw blacks reaching national prominence in a wide range of career fields—science, medicine, business, and the arts. Spirituals and jazz, forms of music that had been developed by blacks, were popular everywhere. A black prizefighter, Joe Louis, took the heavyweight title. Jesse Owens, a black track star, led the United States to victory in the 1936 Olympics, in Berlin. The achievements of these people helped weaken the black stereotype; Owens's wins were doubly important because Adolf Hitler, Germany's Nazi leader, had hoped to use the Olympics as a showcase for his racial theories.

Hitler believed that the Aryan race—basically, white people of northern European stock—was by nature superior to all other races and was destined to conquer and rule them. In his book *Mein Kampf,* he argued:

"Everything that today we admire on this earth—science and art, technique and inventions—is only the creative product of a few peoples and perhaps originally of one race. On them now depends also the existence of this entire culture. If they perish, then the beauty of this earth sinks into the grave with them." His theories led him to vehement racial hatred and ultimately to genocide—the attempt to destroy an entire people, in this case, the Jews, and other "inferior races" of Europe.

World War II pitted the democracies of Western Europe and the United States against Nazi Germany and other fascist states. The war was fought with ideas as well as guns, and the democracies sought to prove the justice of their system. Hitler's brand of racism was strongly opposed in the United States. It also served as a lesson of where unchecked racial hatred might lead.

The combination of growing black racial consciousness, the increasing prominence of blacks, and opposition to Hitler's racism created the start of a new racial climate in the United States. In 1941 President Franklin D. Roosevelt prohibited racial discrimination in defense industries and in government. More than one million blacks served in the armed forces during the war. Until 1944 segregation was still the rule in the service, but a number of blacks attained high rank and honors. They included Benjamin O. Davis, the first black general.

But despite these changes, racial prejudice still ran strong in the United States. The outbreak of World War II also revived the demand for workers in the industrial cities of the North and the Midwest. The black migration from the South, which had halted during the Depression, resumed, and once again blacks met with stiff opposition from whites. Housing was short, and riots broke out in several major cities. In Detroit in 1943, in one of the worst riots, twenty-five blacks and nine whites were killed.

The Civil Rights Movement

The early postwar years were a boom time for most of the United States—and a time of setbacks for most blacks. As more blacks moved to cities in search of jobs, racial violence grew more intense. The small advances that blacks had won in the war years seemed likely to be lost.

The gains were not lost, however. Through the war years many people had become aware of the dangers and injustices of racial prejudice, and they brought pressure on the government to control the situation. In the late 1940s President Harry S. Truman appointed three separate commissions to study the problem of race relations in the areas of political and employment rights, education, and the armed forces. Each commission recommended measures that would give blacks full equality and would protect their rights in the face of prejudice.

The result was a series of laws and court decisions that marked the beginning of the end for the "separate but equal" concept. Truman ordered equal treatment for all races in the armed forces. Federal laws banned lynching. In a series of decisions, the United States Supreme Court outlawed discrimination in housing, interstate bus transportation, and (in the 1954 case *Brown v. Board of Education of Topeka, Kansas*) education.

But outlawing such discrimination was not the same as ending it. Many towns and cities, particularly in the South, were slow to put the new rulings into effect or refused outright to do so. In 1957, for example, nine black students who wanted to enroll in the Little Rock,

Black and white youths staged a sit-in
demonstration at a New York City
Woolworth's store in 1960 to protest
segregated lunch counters in the South.
Unable to find a seat and obviously
unsympathetic to the cause, the woman
at left has a few sharp words
to say to the demonstrators.

*In one of the most memorable 1960s civil rights demonstrations,
a crowd of more than 200,000 lined the edges of the long
reflecting pool in front of the Lincoln Memorial during the
March on Washington for Jobs and Freedom in August 1963.*

Arkansas, high school had to be escorted there by federal troops for their own protection. Transportation and other services remained segregated in many areas.

As the Little Rock incident clearly showed, however, blacks were no longer willing to accept a second-class place in society. Little Rock was just one of many incidents at this time in which blacks openly challenged the concept of white superiority. In 1955 the Reverend Martin Luther King, Jr., led a boycott of city buses in Montgomery, Alabama, after a black woman, Rosa Parks, was arrested there for refusing to give up her seat to a white man. The boycott inspired blacks in other cities and led to a Supreme Court ban on segregation in public transportation in 1956. In 1957 black college students in Greensboro, North Carolina, staged a sit-in at an all-white lunch counter, refusing to move until they were served. Sit-ins thereafter became a popular form of protest in the South. In 1961 protesters dubbed "freedom riders" forced the integration of interstate buses and bus terminals.

The new movement for civil rights gathered strength throughout the 1960s, led by such groups as King's Southern Christian Leadership Conference (SCLC) and the Congress of Racial Equality (CORE). Their protests were nonviolent, but they often met with violent resistance, especially in the South. Police used electric cattle prods and nightsticks to break up the demonstrations. Churches used for meetings were sometimes set on fire. In 1964 three civil rights workers in Philadelphia, Mississippi, were arrested and then released from jail to be killed outright by Ku Klux Klan members.

But for the first time, blacks found widespread support among whites. Many of the 1960s civil rights workers, including two of the three killed in Philadelphia, Mississippi, were white. And the movement brought concrete results—the Twenty-fourth Amendment to the Constitution, which prohibited the poll taxes that had been used in several Southern states to deny blacks the vote; and the Civil Rights Act of 1964, which banned segregation and discrimination in housing, employment, voting, and other areas. These laws were followed by others that were even broader and firmer in their affirmation of black rights. King himself was awarded the Nobel Peace Prize in 1964.

Broad, firm civil rights laws did not guarantee equality, however. The new laws faced the same resistance as previous laws. Some blacks were impatient with the slow progress their people were making, and in the late 1960s, riots—born of dissatisfaction over failure to enforce the laws—broke out in a number of cities.

Some black groups began to advocate taking stronger steps. Groups such as the Black Panthers often clashed with the police. The Black Muslims, a religious group, urged blacks to separate themselves from whites. Other groups concentrated on programs that would help blacks gain political and economic clout—"black power." These groups sponsored voter registration drives and promoted black-run schools, businesses, and social programs. "Black is beautiful" was a slogan that summed up the desire for a new, positive self-image for blacks.

Many of these efforts met with success. But they also aroused fear and prejudice in whites, even among some whites who had supported earlier civil rights efforts. These people found the militancy of groups like the Panthers alarming, and they began to harden their attitudes toward all black protestors, Panthers or not. In some areas blacks met with a white "backlash"—an increase in prejudice provoked by the civil rights movement. In 1968, for example, Governor George Wallace of Alabama attracted significant support when he campaigned for the presidency on an openly segregationist platform. But perhaps the darkest moment in this era was the assassination of Martin Luther King, Jr., by a white man. King was shot in Memphis, Tennessee, on April 4, 1968.

King's death touched off riots in more than thirty cities—riots that left forty-six people dead and over twenty-five hundred injured. But after soldiers had brought the situation under control, the incident was seen to have had a sobering effect on both sides. Blacks and whites alike were genuinely grieved by King's death. No new black leader of his stature emerged. But through the 1970s blacks continued to make steady progress toward equality, especially in politics.

Black candidates won the support of white as well as black voters and were elected to public office in greater numbers than at any time since Reconstruction—as mayors, councilmen, state and national legislators. In 1984 the Reverend Jesse Jackson mounted a serious challenge for the Democratic presidential nomination. His campaign also served as the focal point of a massive voter registration drive that, its supporters hoped, would make blacks a force to be reckoned with in politics.

Effects of the Civil Rights Movement
That the civil rights movement has improved life for many blacks is clear. Black incomes have risen faster than white incomes in recent years, and blacks are becoming increasingly accepted in business and the professions. Even most Southern communities are now substantially integrated; in Philadelphia, Mississippi, where the Ku Klux Klan killed civil rights workers in 1964, blacks today serve on the city council, the school board, and the police force.

But whether the civil rights movement has ended prejudice against blacks is quite another question. Discriminatory practices are no longer legal, but blacks still face significant barriers to equality.

Today most of these barriers are economic ones. Although blacks live in all parts of the United States, they remain concentrated in the rural South and in the older industrial cities of the North and Midwest. Economic troubles in the 1970s and early 1980s hit all farmers hard; black farmers, however, had less to start with than their white colleagues. Meanwhile, many cities have seen industries and businesses depart for the suburbs, taking jobs with them. Financial strain has also forced many cities to cut social-welfare programs, and there have been cuts in state and federal programs as well.

The result has been an increase in unemployment among blacks, especially black teenagers. With this has come an increase in the number of people living in poverty. Crime and drugs have become major problems in most cities, and while blacks are by no means alone in suffering these ills, their low economic status ensures that they bear the brunt of them. Additionally, the strains of poverty have helped weaken the traditionally strong black family, to the point where the percentage of black families that are headed by single parents is much greater than that of white families.

Partly, this situation is the legacy of years of prejudice. Even when people have the opportunity to advance, it takes years to learn the skills that will permit them to improve their economic position. The problem has been compounded by a sluggish economy—good jobs are already filled by qualified people, and few new jobs are being created.

Affirmative-action programs, which were designed in the 1960s and 70s to give blacks and other minorities preference so they could move up quickly through the ranks in jobs or education, have been challenged in court. Some court rulings have held that these programs are a form of reverse discrimination—they discriminate against qualified whites.

To many people, however, the continuing problems faced by blacks are less a legacy of prejudice than a sign that prejudice persists. It seems clear that in most of the United States, at least, prejudice no longer reaches the extremes that it did in the late 1800s and in the early 1900s. But white attitudes toward black people vary, and prejudice can be found in more than trace amounts.

This, at any rate, was the finding of a survey taken by sociologists at the University of Michigan in the 1970s, not long after the peak of the civil rights movement. The author, Angus Campbell, found that between a fifth and a third of Northern white city-dwellers accepted interracial contact, were sensitive to discrimination, and were sympathetic to black protests. About the same number of people were negative on the subject, some of them openly hostile. In between these two poles were large numbers of people whose attitudes were confused and contradictory—for example, who felt on the one hand that blacks had a right to protest against discrimination, but on the other that sit-ins were unjustified. Whites in the suburbs held similar views.

Most whites, the survey found, had given up the idea that blacks were racially incapable of competing on an equal footing with whites. But they had not accepted the other side of that coin—that the problems faced by blacks must stem from their situation in society. More than half felt that blacks experienced poverty and other problems because they had failed to better themselves—they lacked motivation, not ability or opportunity.

By comparing their results with those of a similar survey taken in 1964, the researchers found that overall prejudice had declined. What their survey couldn't tell, of course, is whether the people interviewed hid deeper prejudice from the poll taker—it is no longer fashionable, as it was a hundred years ago, to air racist views in public.

But even this change in fashion is significant. The black stereotype seems to be weakening, although it is still with us. Blacks have already made enormous strides in overcoming deeply rooted racial prejudice. And the survey takers found added encouragement in the fact that the young people interviewed seemed to have the most open views. If this trend continues, prejudice against blacks will continue to lessen in the years to come.

The Indians—Aliens in Their Own Land

Such of the Goshoots as we saw . . . were small, lean, "scrawny" creatures; in complexion a dull black like the ordinary American Negro; their faces and hands bearing dirt which they had been hoarding and accumulating for months, years, and even generations . . . a silent, sneaking, treacherous-looking race; taking note of everything, covertly, like all the other "Noble Red Men" that we (do not) read about, and betraying no sign on their continences; indolent, everlastingly patient and tireless, like all other Indians; prideless beggars—for if the beggar instinct were left out of the Indian he would not "go," any more than a clock without a pendulum; hungry, always hungry, and yet never refusing anything that a hog would eat, though often eating what a hog would decline; hunters, but having no higher ambition than to kill and eat jackass rabbits, crickets, and grasshoppers, and embezzle carrion from the buzzards and coyotes; savages who, when asked if they have the common Indian belief in a Great Spirit, show a something which almost amounts to emotion, thinking whiskey is referred to. . . .

This bitter condemnation of the Gosiute Indians is from Mark Twain's *Roughing It,* an account of the author's travels in the American West in the mid-1800s. Twain's views were by no means restricted to one tribe, nor was he alone in holding them. The passage he wrote enumerates the main features of a negative stereotype of Indians that has been widely held in the United States:

- Indians are filthy.
- They are treacherous. You can never trust them; they consider it a virtue to lie, and if you turn your back on them they will kill you.
- Indians are lazy people. They prefer to live on handouts, rather than work for a living. Dirt-poor living conditions really do not bother them because they do not aspire to anything better.
- They are notorious drunks who will do anything to get their hands on liquor.

But this thoroughly repulsive picture was not the only stereotype of the Indian that developed. Consider these lines from the poem "The Last of the Taschatas," written by the American poet Joaquin Miller at about the same time that Twain wrote the passage above:

His breast was like a gate of brass,
His brow was like a gather'd storm;
There is no chisell'd stone that has
So stately and complete a form.
In sinew, arm and every part,
In all the galleries of art.

This was the Indian as "noble savage"—an idealized being who lived by the laws of nature; glowing with health, innocent, naturally virtuous, and untroubled by the complexities of European society.

The two pictures could not have been more different, and the fact that they could develop side by side is testimony to the vast ignorance of most whites where Indians were concerned. In fact, the native peoples who

lived in North America when the first European settlers arrived were neither more nor less noble than
whites—they simply belonged to a culture that was totally different from the settlers'. Rather than attempt-
ing to understand that culture, most whites kept their
distance from the Indians and clung to their preconceived views.

As white settlements expanded and came into increasing conflict with Indian groups, it was the negative stereotype that won out. Deep and long-lasting
prejudices developed against Indians, with the result
that they became second-class citizens in their own land.

Early Contacts
The people the early settlers met in the New World were
not a single group—they comprised many different nations. Yet while the newly arrived whites were quick to
distinguish between "friendly" and "hostile" groups,
they tended to lump them all together in speech and
thought. The terms *heathens, pagans, savages,* and *Indians* were used interchangeably to refer to them.*

The early British settlers derived their ideas about
Indians from several sources. The Spanish had already
had considerable contact with native groups, and their
experiences were recounted in English-language books.
In Spain two opposing views on the Indians were argued hotly in the 1500s. One, as outlined by Juan Ginés
de Sepúlveda, held that the Indians were beasts—"lit-

---

*This tendency persists today in the use of the term *Indian*—itself a misno-
mer coined by Christopher Columbus, who thought he had arrived in the
East Indies when he reached America. For this reason, many Indian groups
today prefer to be called "Native Americans"—a term that could be taken
several ways, as it could refer to any person born in the Western Hemisphere.

tle men in whom you will scarcely find traces of humanity." Said Sepúlveda,

> What can you expect from men who were involved in every kind of intemperence and wicked lust and who used to eat human flesh? And don't think that before the arrival of the Christians they were living in quiet and the Saturnian peace of the poets. On the contrary they were making war continuously and ferociously against each other. . . .

This view required that the Indians be brutally subjugated, and in fact brutal treatment and slavery were the fate of most Indians in the Spanish colonies at this time.

The opposite view was championed by Bartolomé de Las Casas, who had come to the New World as a conquistador but then entered the priesthood and became known as the Apostle of the Indians. Las Casas fought long and hard to improve conditions for the Indians. To him, they were by nature good:

> God created these simple people without evil and without guile. They are the most obedient and faithful to their natural lords and to the Christians whom they serve. . . . Nor are they quarrelsome, rancorous, querulous, or vengeful. . . . Surely these people would be the most blessed in the world if only they worshipped the true God.

Las Casas eventually won both the Spanish government and the Roman Catholic church to his way of thinking, and Indian slavery gradually died out in the

Spanish colonies. This did not mean that Indians became the equals of Spaniards, though. Despite their apparent opposition, Las Casas's and Sepúlveda's views had a common thread: both held the Indians to be deficient because they did not follow European ways.

The British and other northern Europeans found support for both Spanish views from other sources. Early explorers to the New World sent back conflicting reports, many of which were collected and published by Richard Hakluyt the Younger in the late 1500s. These books circulated widely. On the one hand, there were tales that painted the native peoples of the Americas as cannibalistic monsters such as this description of the Eskimos: "I think them rather Anthropophagi, or devourers of mans flesh than otherwise: for that there is no flesh of fish which they find dead (smell it never so filthily) but they eate it, as they finde it without any other dressing."

On the other hand were the reports of those who wanted to encourage colonization in the New World. For example, Arthur Barlowe, who journeyed to Roanoke Island in 1584, said, "Wee found the people most gentle, loving, and faithful, void of all guile, and treason, and such as lived after the manner of the golden age."

The "golden age" referred to by Barlowe was a time when, it was widely believed, people had lived in innocence, in harmony with nature and reason. French writers in particular seized on this image and began to portray the Indian as the noble savage. From the late 1500s right into the 1700s, the French writers Montaigne, Rousseau, Voltaire, and Diderot and the British philosopher Locke extolled the virtues of natural "primitive" societies.

These, then, were the pictures of Indians that the early British colonists took to the New World. Not surprisingly, they saw just what they expected to see.

Some of the colonists hoped to convert the "gentle, loving, and faithful" Indians to Christianity and thus improve them—in fact, this was often given as one of the prime motives for founding colonies in the first place. The seal of Massachusetts Bay Colony bore a picture of an Indian and the words "Come over and help us." One of the leading Massachusetts missionaries was John Eliot, who formed settlements of converted "Praying Indians." Even the missionaries didn't want to bring the Indians into their society, however; Eliot recommended that they live "somewhere remote from the English, where they must have the word constantly taught, and government constantly exercised."

Relations between the British and the Indians broke down quickly, however. The Indians saw the British clearing their land and building fortified stockades; British cattle trampled Indian corn. There were bloody Indian uprisings—a massacre in Virginia in 1622 and, in New England, King Philip's War in 1675–76. But these revolts came too late to break the foothold that the colonists had established. After the Virginia uprising the colonists reported that they were relieved because "our hands, which before were tied with gentleness and fair useage, are now set at liberty by the treacherous violence of the savages . . . the way of conquering them is much more easy than of civilizing them."

The notion that came to the fore, then, was that the Indians were treacherous and bloodthirsty savages incapable of "improvement" along European lines. As the colonies expanded, the Indians were pushed back, not drawn into society.

The idea of the noble savage enjoyed a brief revival at the time of the American Revolution, since many of the founders were steeped in the works of philosophers such as Locke, who believed in the natural rationality of humankind. But by this time, whites who had any significant contact with Indians were increasingly few in number. Those who had contact often capitalized on their experiences with horrifying tales. Stories of whites who were captured by Indians and subjected to horrifying brutalities were the popular spine-chillers of the day. And during the Revolution itself, the Indians were the enemy—they fought on the side of the British, who armed them and paid high bounties for American scalps.

Thus, by the end of the eighteenth century, two popular images of Indians were firmly in place. There were "good" Indians—the noble savages, rare holdovers from an earlier golden age. And there were "bad" Indians, savages who tortured and scalped helpless whites. With the new country poised for westward expansion, these images were ominous signs for the future of North America's native peoples.

The Indian Wars

Apart from their differences in race, religion, and customs, the Indians and whites were separated by deep differences in their social systems. The settlers were mostly farmers who believed strongly in the value of owning land and other property. Most Indians were hunters who might range over a territory of thousands of square miles but held property loosely or in common. Thus, to the whites, the Indians had no valid claims to the vast North American wilderness.

This view blended well with others held by whites—

*Indians of many different tribes were welcomed
at the White House by President Andrew Johnson
in 1867. Such gestures of good will did not make up
for endless broken treaties, however, and throughout
most of the nineteenth century whites and Indians
out on the frontier were bitter foes.*

the negative stereotype of Indians, the semiscientific theory that nonwhite races were inferior, the belief that white Americans were a "chosen people" sent to "tame" the wilderness. The result was the conviction that it was the white destiny to settle the new lands "from sea to shining sea." Tribe after tribe lost its hunting grounds to waves of settlers, by sale, treaty, or outright seizure. The game animals the Indians depended on—particularly the great herds of buffalo in the Plains—were killed or driven off by the advancing tide.

From the start the Indians fought back, and for the hundred years from 1790 to 1890 the United States Army met Indian warriors in one bloody conflict after another. Troops led by General "Mad Anthony" Wayne defeated the Miamis in Ohio in 1794. In 1811 in the future state of Indiana, at the hard-fought battle of Tippecanoe, General William Henry Harrison defeated Tecumseh, chief of the Shawnees, and earned himself a reputation that led to the presidency. Andrew Jackson conquered the Creeks in Louisiana in 1814 and subdued the Seminoles in Florida in 1818.

Since it was felt that Indian and white society could not blend, until 1825 the government's policy was that Indians should be restricted to reservations in their original homelands, where they would become farmers. And as white settlements grew, Congress decided that all Indians should be removed to new reservations west of the Mississippi River, where the land was thought to be less hospitable. In many cases the result was fresh outbreaks of fighting.

Indians were at a disadvantage in these fights. They were often poorly armed and were outnumbered, and the various tribes seldom formed alliances to oppose the whites. One by one the tribes of the Midwest—the Black Hawk, Sac, and Fox—were defeated. Meanwhile, in the

South, the Cherokees were forced from their land and ordered to march to Indian territory in what is now Oklahoma—a journey that became known as the Trail of Tears. They were joined along the way by the Choctaws and the Creeks. A second Seminole war, led by Chief Osceola, broke out in 1835 and dragged on for seven years before the Indians were finally defeated.

It was not long before white settlers were moving beyond the Mississippi and into the West, and the Indians were pressured again. During the Mexican War of 1846–48, United States troops stormed the adobe dwellings of the Pueblos in New Mexico. And fighting along the frontier did not stop during the Civil War, although both North and South bid for Indian support with offers of land and other rewards. There were tragedies on both sides. The Santee Sioux killed more than eight hundred whites in Minnesota. In Colorado in 1864 soldiers killed three hundred Cheyennes, including women and children, who had tried to surrender.

In the Far West it was the soldiers who often found themselves outnumbered by the Indians. Their battles were reported to the populated East, and Indian-fighters quickly attained the status of mythical heroes. There was "Portugee" Phillips, who rode through a blinding blizzard to bring help to Fort Phil Kearny in Wyoming, besieged by the Sioux in 1867. There was General George Crook, who crushed two Apache uprisings in the Southwest—the second, which lasted from 1882 to 1886, led by Geronimo. And, of course, there was General George Armstrong Custer, who fell to Sitting Bull's Sioux warriors at the Battle of Little Big Horn in 1876. Less widely publicized were other aspects of Indian-white relations—the fact, for example, that the Apache uprising of 1882 was sparked by cheating on the part of government Indian agents.

The aftermath of the battle at Wounded Knee,
South Dakota, where over three hundred Sioux, many
of them unarmed women and children, were killed

One of the last—and most tragic—episodes of violence occurred at Wounded Knee, in South Dakota, in 1890. The Sioux, prompted by a medicine man's prophecy, gathered to perform "ghost dances" and await the coming of a messiah who would restore the Indians to their former status. The government saw the gathering as preparation for war and ordered the arrest of Sitting Bull. Sioux warriors sprang to their chief's defense, Sitting Bull was shot, and in the ensuing fray nearly three hundred Sioux, many of them unarmed women and children, were killed.

The Indian Image
The glorified accounts of Indian fighting served to confirm the belief that Indians were bloodthirsty savages. To the bulk of Americans, living in the East, Indians were a distant enemy that stood in the way of progress and expansion. And to the pioneers who sought to settle the West, warring Indians were a daily fear. But gradually, once the native Americans were safely placed on distant lands that no white person wanted, Indians began to be seen as semimythical creatures.

A new version of the noble-savage myth glorified famous Indians of the past. Perhaps the best-known purveyor of this image was James Fenimore Cooper, whose novels were written in the 1820s and remained popular well into the 1900s. Cooper had little if any contact with Indians and presented both the "noble" and "savage" stereotypes in his books. Henry Wadsworth Longfellow's famous poem *The Song of Hiawatha* (1855) was another product of the vogue for romanticizing the Indian.

These glorified clichés did little to promote understanding between the two races. And as these writers saw it, nobility was no help to Indians. Most of the writers who took this view stressed that the Indians were doomed to vanish in the face of civilization. For example, Oliver Wendell Holmes contended in the mid-1800s that Indians would become extinct if they could not run free—"and so the red-crayon sketch is rubbed out, and the canvas is ready for a picture of manhood a little more like God's own image."

By the late 1800s mythical Indians had become stock characters in a new kind of popular fiction—the Western. The old images of "good" and "bad" Indians were trotted out again and again in dime novels. There were a few trustworthy Indians, typified by the Lone Ranger's faithful Tonto, who helped whites. And there were evil, treacherous Indians who swooped down to attack defenseless wagon trains with murderous yells. Popular shows helped spread the myths—Buffalo Bill's Wild West Show, for example, presented matinee reenactments of Custer's Last Stand. And as film and, later, television came on the scene, these stereotyped images were confirmed.

Whites believed the Indian stereotypes presented in Westerns because, in most cases, fictional Indians were the only ones they ever saw. By 1900 the total Indian population had dropped from about one million before contact with Europeans to about three hundred thousand, partly because of the wars but even more because of illness. Where they had come in contact with whites, the Indians had often been destroyed by diseases such as smallpox, measles, and tuberculosis, to which they had no natural immunity. And as their numbers had decreased, the strength of the tribes had been whittled away.

One by one, the tribes had been consigned to reservations in strange and often hostile places. The government gave the Indians farming tools and rations and

This Indian family, photographed at the
Pine Ridge Sioux reservation in 1898,
wears fashions of the period—except
for grandmother (seated) who has kept
her traditional Sioux costume.

set up schools, and whites in general expected that the Indians would gradually see the benefits of "civilization" and give up their traditional ways. But the change from a free way of life to the restrictions of the reservation brought despair. Social problems—poverty and alcholism in particular—were severe.

Prejudice prevented whites from seeing the social causes of these problems; rather, the Indians themselves were held responsible. Thus the "good" and "bad" Indians of the Westerns were seen as belonging to the historical past. When whites thought about the actual Indians who lived on reservations, the image that emerged was that of the "Goshoots" described by Mark Twain—creatures to be viewed with contempt. This view found support in the pseudoscientific theories about race that held sway in the late 1800s and early 1900s. For example, a popular book of the 1800s, *Types of Mankind*, by Josiah Clark Nott and George Robin Gliddon, asserted that Indians were "colored vermin" and that "it is vain to talk of civilizing them. You might as well attempt to change the nature of a buffalo."

With such views in the mainstream, whites often ignored treaties and continued to deal unfairly with the Indians. Right into the 1900s Indians were shunted from one reservation to another, forced to sell or lease their land for next to nothing, or simply cheated out of it. In 1905, for example, on the grounds that the relevant treaties had never been brought to the Senate for a vote, the government sold to white settlers and speculators 7.5 million acres that had been ceded to California Indians.

In its treatment of the Indians, the United States government acted in direct opposition to its principles of equality and human rights. The motive may have been greed for land. But the justifications offered were racial. In *The Winning of the West* President Theodore Roosevelt summed up the prevailing view near the turn of the century:

"I don't go as far as to think that the only good Indians are the dead Indians, but I believe nine out of every ten are, and I shouldn't inquire too closely into the case of the tenth. The most vicious cowboy has more moral principle than the average Indian."

The Indians Today

Not all whites shared Theodore Roosevelt's view, and the Indians were not without defenders. One of the most moving accounts of their mistreatment was the 1881 book *A Century of Dishonor*, by Helen Hunt Jackson, who also wrote the novel *Ramona*. But by and large, pleas for better treatment of the Indians fell on deaf ears.

By the 1960s, then, the Indians stood at the bottom of the social and economic scale in the United States. The average Indian family had an annual income of fifteen hundred dollars, compared to the national average of five thousand dollars. About 40 percent of Indians were unemployed, compared to 3 percent of the national population. Housing was well below minimum standards—more than half of Indian families had no running water, and death rates from infectious diseases such as pneumonia and influenza were double the national average. About 80 percent of Indians lived on reservations, where they attempted to make a meager living by farming, raising livestock, or working in tribal-owned businesses such as sawmills. But life was seldom better for those who left to find work in cities.

These conditions were the legacy of the whites' earlier treatment of the Indians and of continuing attempts to force the Indians to accept "superior" white ways. In education, for example, the government's policy was to send Indian children to boarding schools run by the Bureau of Indian Affairs, where they were taught from white texts that ignored their culture or mentioned it only in negative terms. The result was that, separated from their families and confronted with material they could not relate to, more than half of Indian children dropped out of school before completing their education. In the 1960s the average Indian had five years of schooling, compared to ten for most Americans.

In 1924 Indians had been granted citizenship, and from that time on there had been several attempts to reform the reservation system. But these attempts were on the whole misguided and ineffective. In the 1950s, for example, Congress called for a policy of "termination" in Indian affairs. "Termination" meant ending federal services and freeing the tribes from government supervision, so that they could be drawn into white society. The Menominee of Wisconsin were one of twelve tribes to be "terminated"; their reservation became a county, and the tribe took control of local mill operations.

The "termination" policy was a failure—it ignored the fact that many Indians preferred traditional tribal governments and values to those of white society. To these Indians the chief benefit of the reservation was that it provided a place where traditions and values could be maintained. They also felt that the federal government was obligated to provide certain services in exchange for the vast amounts of land it had obtained from the Indians. In 1975, the government reestablished the Menominee reservation and the Indians regained their tribal rights and status.

New policies came to the fore in the 1960s, a time

of increasing concern about poverty and minority rights. As the black civil rights movement drew national attention, Indians also began to speak up. New Indian organizations such as the National Congress of American Indians and the National Indian Youth Council focused not only on past injustices but on modern ones— demands on the Indians to give up water, mineral, and development rights to their land, for example.

In the late 1960s and early 1970s, a number of groups staged dramatic demonstrations. One group briefly seized Alcatraz Island in San Francisco Bay, the site of an abandoned federal prison, and claimed it as Indian territory. Another group briefly occupied the office of the Bureau on Indian Affairs in Washington, D.C. In 1973 members of the American Indian Movement (AIM) took over a church building in Wounded Knee, South Dakota, holding eleven hostages. Federal authorities besieged the building for seventy days. By the end of the incident, two Indians had been killed, at least nine other people had been wounded, and most of Wounded Knee was a shambles. In a larger and more peaceful demonstration, dubbed "the longest walk," in 1978, many Indians took part in a five-month march from San Francisco to Washington, D.C.

Such demonstrations drew attention to the Indians' problems, but perhaps more effective were a number of court cases. Many involved claims to land. On the grounds that past treaties were illegal or improperly enforced, Indians have claimed parts of Connecticut, Maine, Massachusetts, New York, Rhode Island, and South Carolina. In several cases they have won money or some amount of land. Other cases have focused on fishing rights and the control of natural resources.

Some people who oppose these claims have proposed limiting tribal rights or canceling past treaties with

In 1978 Indians made "the longest walk," a five-month march from San Francisco to Washington, D.C., to draw attention to the injustices they suffered.

the Indians. But on the whole, since the 1960s the Indians have received a more sympathetic hearing from government and private citizens alike than at any other time in history. This is partly the effect of the concern for ecology and of the counterculture movement that developed in the late 1960s. The industrialism and emphasis on individual success that mark white society were seen to have devastating effects, destroying natural resources and polluting the environment. People began to appreciate traditional Indian values that stressed respect for nature and tribal, rather than individual, benefits.

In the films and fiction of recent years, Indians have often been presented as heroes, while whites are the villains. One public-service television announcement shows an Indian weeping silent tears at the sight of industrial pollution. This new image itself is a stereotype—the Indian as a wise, saddened critic of white society. But accurate or not, the change is a hopeful sign. It indicates that whites are becoming aware of the prejudice with which they have treated Indians in the past, and that they are at last becoming more tolerant of the Indians' choice to live according to their own traditions.

6 | The Asian Americans

> . . . for ways that are dark
> And for tricks that are vain
> The heathen Chinee is peculiar.

These lines from the poem "The Heathen Chinee," by Bret Harte, sum up the strong feelings that Chinese immigrants encountered when they began to arrive in large numbers on the West Coast of the United States in the 1800s. Other Asian immigrants, coming after the Chinese, encountered much the same fear and hatred. Like other racial minorities, the Asians were victims of prejudice.

The negative stereotype that developed about Asians was similar to the stereotypes of blacks and Indians in some ways, but it differed in important ways, too. Asians in general have made such enormous strides in overcoming prejudice that the stereotype is far less widely held now than it was even fifty years ago. But it resurfaces from time to time. The basic features are:

- Asians are sneaky and deceitful people who cannot be trusted.
- They are intelligent to the point of being crafty, and they use their intelligence to plot against white people.
- Asians are evil. They have no moral sense; Chinatowns are places of vice and corruption.
- They are clannish, keeping to themselves and forming secret societies that usually have criminal goals.

• Asians are dirty; Chinese neighborhoods are unsanitary and often ridden with disease.

In fact, the Chinese, who were among the earliest Asian immigrants in the United States, were for the most part quiet, sober, frugal, and hardworking—all qualities that the American republic glorified in its own citizens. They worked at hard jobs for low wages and still managed to send money back to their families in China. Their chief goal was to prosper and then to return to their homeland.

But where the Chinese were concerned, these very qualities were seen as evidence against them. The fact that they were quiet was proof of their natural deceitfulness. The fact that they worked for low wages and saved their money was proof that they planned to drain the United States of its money and resources—and so on. Asians, in short, were a danger to the United States, the "Yellow Peril" that might bring the country to its knees. How they came to be regarded as such a threat is a fascinating chapter in American history.

The Chinese—
First Immigrants from the East
To Americans, Asia has always had an air of mystery about it—the exotic Orient. And no country embodied that mystery as much as China, the fabled Cathay of Marco Polo and Kubla Khan. China's history goes back thousands of years, and for centuries it was one of the most advanced civilizations on earth. But that civilization was almost unknown to people in Western Europe and the Americas. It was separated from them by vast distances, by oceans, mountains, and deserts.

For centuries the Chinese preferred to keep contact with the outside world to a minimum. They feared that

Western countries would sooner or later try to rule over China, as they had done in India and the Philippines, and so the Chinese placed stiff restrictions on trade with the West. It wasn't until 1842, when the British defeated the Chinese in the Opium War and forced them to open more ports and to relax restrictions, that trade increased.

Sleek American clipper ships soon began to call at Chinese ports for cargoes of tea, silk, and porcelain. And the sailors on these ships brought with them tales of mountains of gold in their homeland—the gold that had been discovered at Sutter's Mill in California in 1849. The Chinese saw America as a land of opportunity, a place where they could become wealthy in a short time and then return to their families in China. By the hundreds, they began to make the seven-thousand-mile voyage east to California. Many did so at great risk—until the 1860s, leaving China without the government's permission was a crime punishable by death.

These early Chinese immigrants were mostly men from the working classes; the educated and wealthy Chinese saw no need to risk their government's wrath by leaving the country. The immigrants had no knowledge of English or of American customs. Usually they signed on with a labor contractor and worked under a Chinese foreman who had some knowledge of English and could arrange to find work. Thus bands of contract "coolie" workers began to appear in the West. They worked on farms and in mines and factories, and they helped build the transcontinental railway.

These bands of Chinese workers were often in demand because they worked quickly and efficiently and for considerably lower wages than white workers. Many Chinese also struck out on their own, as miners or in services that the mining towns needed. They were quick

This nineteenth century lithograph shows the typical "welcome" extended to newly-arrived Chinese immigrants in San Francisco.

to see that, with few women around, the Western towns and mining camps needed such services as laundries and restaurants. And they were willing to take servants' positions and other jobs that white workers scorned.

By 1870 there were more than sixty-three thousand Chinese in America, all but forty-five hundred of them men. But despite their industry, the Chinese found no welcome in the United States. This was partly because their features and their customs were startling to American eyes. Not only did they, with their deeper skin tone and Asian features, look odd to the Americans, but they dressed differently and wore their hair in long single braids, or queues. Their language was unintelligible, and their religion (chiefly Buddhist) was branded as heathen.

The Chinese initially made little effort to change their customs or adapt to America because they assumed that they would soon return to China. A Chinese man could not cut off his queue, for example, because he was required by Chinese law to wear his hair that way and could not return to China without it. Cutting off queues became a favorite prank in America; whites would sneak up behind a Chinese, snip, and run, laughing at the rage and grief their act provoked. Usually these pranksters had no idea that their joke had doomed the victim to exile.

But appearance and customs were not solely responsible for the deep prejudice the Chinese encountered. The presence of the industrious coolie bands sparked a deep fear in some Americans—the fear that they would lose their own jobs.

This fear was strongest in California, where most of the Chinese lived. But it emerged elsewhere, too. When workers at a shoe factory in North Adams, Massachusetts, struck in 1870, the factory owner fired them and imported a group of Chinese workers from San Francisco. The townspeople stoned the Chinese as they disembarked from the train that brought them to North Adams, but soon the new workers were producing more shoes for lower wages than the white workers had. Other factory owners followed suit. Manufacturers began to talk of the virtually limitless supply of cheap labor from China. The Chinese, some people said, would become America's new underclass—a "yellow proletariat" of migrant workers that would replace slaves in agriculture and white workers (who often demanded higher wages and better working conditions) in factories.

White workers reacted, and they found spokesmen for their fears. One was Henry George, who had been born in Philadelphia, had gone to California in a fruitless attempt to get ahead, and became widely known as a labor reformer. George saw in the Chinese the seeds of destruction for the United States; land and factory owners, he was convinced, would use the Chinese to displace the American worker and thus end the spirit of free enterprise that had built the country. Another spokesman with similar views was Denis Kearney, an Irish sailor who founded the American Workingmen's Party in California. Kearney was a thunderous orator. And the press gave wide coverage to his anti-Chinese speeches, which always ended with the call "The Chinese must go!"

These and other speakers brought anti-Chinese feelings to a head, and violence was the result. In incidents throughout the late 1870s, Chinese were stoned, robbed, driven from their homes, and murdered in towns in California, Wyoming, and Oregon. In 1880 a major riot destroyed every Chinese home and business

A cartoon from the late 1870s, captioned "We don't want any cheap-labor foreigners intruding upon us native-born citizens," pointed out the intolerance of Americans who were not far removed from immigrant status themselves.

*A street thronged with men in San Francisco's
Chinatown in the late 1800s. Since few
Chinese women emigrated to the United States,
Chinese communities around the turn of the
century were nearly all-male societies.*

in Denver, Colorado. The Chinese had no recourse in these incidents. They were not United States citizens, and—although a treaty between the United States and China assured them good treatment—China was powerless to intervene.

In 1882 Congress, bowing to pressure from voters chiefly in the West and the South, voted to suspend immigration from China for ten years. The Chinese Exclusion Act of 1882 was followed by other, similar acts that banned or severely limited Chinese immigration through the 1920s. Chinese could still enter the country if they were the children of United States citizens. But few could meet this condition. Chinese immigrants were not allowed to become naturalized citizens—that is, they could not become citizens by choice. Thus the only Chinese-American citizens were those who had been born in the United States. And since most of the immigrants had not brought their wives, there were very few Chinese Americans who were born in America.

Still, the Chinese found ways to keep coming. The largest Chinese population was in San Francisco, and in 1906 a massive earthquake and fire destroyed not only San Francisco's Chinatown but also the government birth records. After the earthquake many Chinese claimed to have been born in America, and they sent for their "children"—people who were often no relation at all—in China. Immigration authorities held these "paper sons," as they were called, for weeks in dismal detention facilities while they grilled them in detail on their family histories. But most had memorized enough details about their "paper fathers" to pass the exam and gain entry.

As before, most of the immigrants were men. In fact, around the turn of the century the ratio of Chinese-American men to women was greater than twenty-five to one. This meant that most Chinese could not marry and start families, a situation that helped keep them separate from the rest of society. The Chinese lived apart, mostly in the Chinatowns of various large cities. Because they could not be sure of equal treatment under American law, they tended to rely on their own organizations—family clans and secret societies called tongs—for law enforcement, charity, and other social services. The tongs were often involved in illegal activities, and prostitution, drugs, and gambling were commonplace in the Chinatowns of the late 1800s. So was poverty. Most of the Chinese who had dreamed of making a fortune in America and returning to their homeland as wealthy men were unable to afford even the passage back.

The anti-immigration forces, of course, used conditions in the Chinatowns as ammunition in their fight. They did not see that prejudice and economic factors kept the Chinese separate and caused most of the problems in Chinese areas. Rather, ignoring the fact that many of the clients in the gambling halls, opium dens, and brothels of the Chinatowns were white, they claimed that vice and poverty stemmed naturally from the Chinese character. White women were warned never to go even to a Chinese laundry alone, for fear they would be kidnapped.

Ironically, few of the Chinese immigrants would have remained in the United States if they had not encountered prejudice. Harassed and held back at every turn, they were unable to achieve their goal of earning a sum of money and returning home. Thus they were forced to make permanent homes in the United States. Gradually, however, conditions among the Chinese Americans began to change.

Three factors were important in changing them. First, the small number of Chinese women in the United States produced daughters as well as sons, and the imbalance in the ratio of men to women grew smaller. In 1930 immigration laws were changed to allow some Chinese wives to join their husbands, and the laws were loosened further in the 1940s. By this time there were a bit fewer than three men to each woman. This meant that more Chinese Americans were able to start families. At the same time many of the earlier immigrants, the stranded single men, died out. As the character of Chinese neighborhoods changed and became more family-oriented, vice declined and the tongs lost their power. Rather than being places to avoid, Chinatowns became tourist attractions.

The second factor was an improvement in economic conditions. Relying on hard work and their own credit organizations, the Chinese were able to make successes of many business ventures. In the 1940s, World War II created new opportunities in factories outside the Chinatowns. The Chinese moved into new lines of work and new neighborhoods.

The third factor was the great emphasis that Chinese Americans traditionally placed on education. Parents worked hard and scrimped to pay for their children's education, and more and more Chinese graduated from college and entered the professions, usually in the sciences. The percentage of Chinese Americans who were in the professions rose dramatically from less than 3 percent in 1930 to 18 percent in 1960—greater than the percentage of whites.

As a result of all these factors, Chinese Americans today have higher incomes and hold higher-status jobs than Americans in general. As they have become more successful economically, they have moved from the old Chinese neighborhoods and mixed more and more with white society. Prejudice against them has grown less and less. But occasionally it still flares up. For example, in 1982 two Detroit men were charged with beating a Chinese to death for the simple fact of his race. The Chinese have made enormous strides in overcoming prejudice—but prejudice is tenacious, and it dies hard.

The Japanese—Held Prisoner

At the same time that the Chinese were finding new opportunities in the factories of World War II, another group of Asians was encountering one of the blackest examples of prejudice in United States history. These were the Japanese.

Until the mid-1800s, Japan was perhaps even more isolated and shrouded in mystery than China. In 1853 Commodore Perry brought a fleet of United States fighting ships into Tokyo Bay and forced the Japanese to increase trade with America. In the years following that incident, Japan became openly pro-American. English was taught in Japanese schools, Benjamin Franklin was held up as a model for Japanese children to follow, and the United States was described as a paradise on earth.

Small wonder, then, that children who had been raised in this atmosphere wanted to go to the United States. Small numbers of Japanese immigrated throughout the late 1800s, and the numbers increased sharply after the first Chinese exclusion acts were passed. Like the Chinese, most of the immigrants were young men—often younger sons who had no prospects of inheriting land—who planned to earn a set sum of money and return home. And like the Chinese, they found this goal harder to achieve than they had imagined. Fewer than half of the Japanese who left their country for the United States in the 1880s and 1890s ever returned.

In America the Japanese found jobs easily, mostly in California. They were ambitious and hardworking, and the exclusion of the Chinese had created a need for laborers who would accept low pay and long hours. Close to half of the Japanese found work in agriculture, and up until the early 1900s, many were able to buy or rent farms of their own. Others worked in mines, mills, and factories or as servants. They were so industrious that when they were paid for piecework rather than by the hour, they often earned more than American workers.

But as the Japanese began to succeed, Americans saw them as competition. Farmers, workers, and business owners pressed for legislation that would halt the Japanese success. In 1908 the United States and Japan drew up the Gentlemen's Agreement, under which Japan strictly limited the number of its citizens that would be allowed to go to the United States. The families of those who were already there were allowed to join them, however; so after this time many Japanese immigrants were women. Some were "picture brides," who were chosen by photograph and married by proxy (that is, with someone else standing in for the bridegroom) before they left for their new homes.

As their families joined them, the Japanese began to put down roots in the United States. But other laws held them back. In 1913, for example, California passed a law that forbade aliens to hold land. Since, like other Asian immigrants, the Japanese could not become citizens, they were prevented from buying farms.

The Japanese also found themselves victims of the prejudice that existed against the Chinese. To most

Americans, the Chinese and Japanese were indistinguishable. The Japanese were just another aspect of the Yellow Peril that threatened the United States. And in the case of Japan, the threat was twofold. Not only were the immigrants seen as a danger, but Japan itself was becoming a strong military power. There were fears of a war in the Pacific. Meanwhile, the discrimination encountered by Japanese in the United States insulted the Japanese government, and relations between the two countries deteriorated.

Faced with prejudice and discrimination, however, the Japanese reacted differently than the Chinese. Rather than retiring to their own enclosed communities, they argued for their rights—and often won. When they were excluded from labor unions, they formed their own associations and obtained fair contracts. They held out for equal pay with white workers in agriculture, too, and were for the most part successful. Employers were generally happy to pay fair wages because the Japanese proved to be such good workers. And the strong tradition of family values that the immigrants had brought with them from Japan kept the crime rate among them extremely low.

By the 1930s the Japanese held an important place in the economy of the West, especially California. Like the Chinese, they were beginning to advance into new fields through education and to seek acceptance in society generally. But the events of World War II proved a disastrous setback for them.

On December 7, 1941, Japan launched a surprise bombing raid on the United States naval forces at Pearl Harbor, in Hawaii. Rumors spread immediately that the attackers had been helped by Japanese Americans on the islands, who were said to have cut arrows pointing toward Pearl Harbor in the sugarcane fields and blocked traffic so that United States servicemen could not get to their posts. The rumors were false, but they spread quickly. There were fears that the next attack might come on the mainland of the United States, perhaps in California.

The FBI took into custody about fifteen hundred Japanese Americans who were thought to have close ties with military leaders in Japan. The Japanese community itself supported this move. But meanwhile, the press and politicians began to whip up anti-Japanese feeling. "The Japanese in California should be under armed guard to the last man and woman right now—and to hell with habeas corpus," wrote the syndicated columnist Westbrook Pegler.

Increasingly, in many people's eyes, the Japanese were judged guilty by association. All Japanese, regardless of their beliefs or politics, were seen as potential saboteurs. And on February 20, 1942, President Franklin D. Roosevelt ordered that all Japanese Americans—whether aliens or citizens, born in Japan or America—be moved inland from their homes near the West Coast.

Supporters of the plan asserted that it was necessary because there was no way to distinguish loyal from disloyal Japanese Americans. They were too different from whites—including German and Italian Americans, whose homelands were also at war with the United States—and couldn't be trusted. California Attorney General Earl Warren, later chief justice of the United States Supreme Court, said, "We believe that when we are dealing with members of the Caucasian race we have methods that will test the loyalty of them. . . . But when we deal with the Japanese we are in an entirely different field and we cannot form any opinion that we believe to be sound." In fact, this argument was

*Members of the Mochida family
awaiting an evacuation bus that
will take them to a detention
camp further inland, photographed
by Dorothea Lange, May 1942.*

nothing more than a restatement of the old prejudicial stereotype: Orientals were inscrutable (hard to understand) and evil by nature.

In response, the Japanese Americans stated their loyalty to the United States and pleaded for just treatment, but announced that they were willing to cooperate as a patriotic duty. The western portions of California, Oregon, and Washington were designated "exclusion areas," and, neighborhood by neighborhood, Japanese were ordered to sell or store their possessions, close their businesses, and prepare for evacuation. Taking only what they could carry, they were sent by bus and train to detention camps that had quickly been set up nearby. When the western parts of the three states had been cleared of Japanese, evacuation began in the eastern parts. In all, about 110,000 people were forced to move.

Larger, more permanent camps were set up in Utah, Arizona, Wyoming, Arkansas, and California, and the Japanese were moved again. In these camps they lived in large barracks, often without running water. Food was provided, but the allowance for it was just forty-five cents per day per person. Workers at the camps were paid a minimal sum—nineteen dollars a month for professionals, sixteen dollars for skilled workers, and twelve dollars for unskilled workers. In general the Japanese were treated humanely, but this did not make up for their loss of liberty and livelihood.

Over time, attempts were made to move the evacuees out of the camps and into new homes away from the West Coast. Those who were citizens were the first to go. Jobs and homes were found for them in places as far-flung as New York and Chicago, and about thirty-five thousand Japanese were relocated in this way. College students were also allowed to leave. In 1943

Japanese were allowed once again to serve in the military, and many seized this chance to prove their loyalty. Then, in January 1945, exclusion ended. By the time Japan surrendered on August 15, 1945, many Japanese had already begun to return to their homes.

Often they found that their possessions had been lost or stolen, and their businesses had vanished. The financial cost to the Japanese was estimated at $400 million. And resentment against them was still high in some areas. But many people felt that the Japanese Americans had proved their loyalty, and after the war they seemed to overcome the obstacles in their paths in leaps and bounds. Having lost their old businesses, they turned to new fields and were successful. By 1970 their average family income was about a third higher than the national average.

The Other Asian Americans
In many ways the Chinese and Japanese paved the way for immigrants from other Asian countries—the Philippines, Korea, and the countries of Southeast Asia. Yet people from these countries have met many of the same prejudices encountered by the Chinese and Japanese.

The Philippines, which had been ruled by Spain, became a United States possession in 1898, at the end of the Spanish-American War. The people of the islands, Filipinos, were Malays who spoke Spanish as well as their own languages. But from the time that the United States took over the government of the islands, schools taught English, American history, and the principles of democracy.

Filipino immigration began on a large scale in the 1920s, when restrictions on Japanese immigration had created a shortage of field workers for West Coast farms. Like earlier Asian immigrants, the Filipinos were largely

young single men who did not plan to stay in the United
States—they sought only to make enough money to set
themselves up comfortably in their homeland. They
worked mostly as unskilled migrant farm workers, us-
ing the same contract labor arrangements as the other
immigrants, and they were often poorly paid. One study
in the late 1920s showed that only black and Mexican
workers were paid less than Filipinos. In cities, meanwhile, they found only low-paying jobs, as busboys,
dishwashers, and servants.

The Filipinos were faced with the same prejudicial
attitudes that had confronted other Asians. The prejudice emerged in job opportunities, housing, and education, and it prevented many from achieving their goal
of returning home wealthy. Thus they were forced to
stay, while their hopes turned to bitter disappointment. In the late 1920s there were anti-Filipino riots on
the West Coast, and laws that excluded the Japanese
and Chinese from owning property or marrying whites
were extended to cover Filipinos as well.

The Filipinos' sense of disappointment was perhaps greater than that of other Asians because they had
been taught to admire the American ideals of democracy, justice, and equality. Carlos Bulosan, a Filipino
immigrant who wrote about his people during the 1930s,
described their feelings this way: "Western people are
brought up to regard Orientals or colored people as inferior, but the mockery of it all is that Filipinos are taught
to regard Americans as our equals. Adhering to American ideals, living American life, these are contributory
to our feeling of equality. The terrible truth in America
shatters the Filipino's dream of fraternity."

In 1946 the Philippines gained independence. At the
same time, Filipinos were allowed to become naturalized United States citizens, but an annual quota of one

hundred immigrants was set. This law remained in effect until 1965, when Congress decided that an immigrant's job and family ties, rather than national origin, should determine whether the immigrant gained admittance.

The change in the immigration laws sparked a wave of fresh immigration from the Philippines. Since 1970 more people have moved to the United States from the Philippines than from any other country except Mexico. Many of the new immigrants were educated and skilled workers, but on the whole they have not found jobs that matched their training. How deeply prejudice against them runs is not clear, since the problems they have faced have not received the attention given to the problems of some other minority groups.

Along with the increase in Filipino immigration, after 1965 came an increase in the numbers of immigrants from other Asian countries. Many of these people were refugees from the political turmoil in Korea and in Vietnam, Cambodia, and other Southeast Asian countries. In the 1970s, during and after the Vietnam War, about 226,000 Vietnamese left their country for the United States.

Charitable groups helped many of these people find jobs and homes in areas around the country, and this eased some of the impact of their move. But some communities were still hard pressed; at one point, in 1979, San Francisco received Southeast Asian refugees at a rate of twenty-five hundred a month. On the whole the new Asian immigrants are moving quickly to establish themselves in their new homeland. Like the Chinese before them, many have gone into business for themselves, especially in the food service industry. And they place the same high priority on education shown by other Asian-American groups.

So far they have faced less discrimination than the other Asians. But prejudice can still be seen in some areas, especially where the new immigrants are starting to compete for jobs with white workers. For example, Southeast Asians who set up as commercial shrimp fishermen along the Gulf Coast have met stiff resistance from established fishermen in the area. And there have been a few instances of hostility between the new immigrants and blacks and other minority groups. One possible reason is that these groups, being low on the social scale, feel most vulnerable to a threat against their jobs.

Like other Asians, too, the Southeast Asians remain a group outside the mainstream of American society, poorly understood by the majority. Earlier Asian immigrants, more than any other group, overcame enormous prejudice. It is to be hoped that the most recent Asian immigrants will have an easier path before them.

7 Hispanic Americans

Ever since Europeans first came in contact with people from other parts of the world, scientists have looked for hard-and-fast, biological rules by which to classify races. What they have learned is that the genetic factors that make one group of people different from another are so complex as to defy easy catagorization. The concept of race is based as much on social beliefs as on physical differences—if one group of people is perceived as different by the majority, the majority will most likely consider that group a separate race.

This is the case with Hispanic Americans, the Spanish-speaking people who form the fastest-growing minority in the United States today. Hispanic Americans are not a single group; they hail from Mexico, Puerto Rico, Cuba, and nearly every other part of Central and South America. Racially, their backgrounds are varied and mixed. The Spanish who conquered and settled the New World did not adhere to the strict bans on racial intermarriage that held in the English-speaking colonies, so Hispanic Americans may count among their ancestors Spaniards, Indians, and blacks who were brought as slaves to the Caribbean.

Legally, Hispanics in the United States have generally been classified as white. But in the eyes of many people, they have been considered a separate—and inferior—race. According to this view, the stereotyped Hispanic has the following traits:

- Hispanics are lazy. They prefer to put off work until *mañana*—tomorrow—and spend today taking a *siesta* in the shade.

- Physically, they are best suited for hard manual labor. Mexicans, for example, do not mind stooping in the fields all day because they are short anyway.
- Hispanics are irresponsible. They have no desire to better themselves and do not mind living in poverty, even in filth.
- "Good" Hispanics are like docile, happy children. If they are treated with an iron hand, they will be content to do as they are told.
- "Bad" Hispanics are vicious criminals—*banditos* in the past, delinquents and drug runners today.
- All Hispanics, good and bad, have uncontrollable tempers, due to their mixture of hot Spanish and savage Indian blood.

The contradictions in the stereotype are obvious—Hispanics are "lazy" but also work long hours at hard jobs whites shun; they are hot-tempered but at the same time "docile." The stereotype also ignores some important facts. These supposedly irresponsible people traditionally have had some of the strongest families—and the lowest divorce rates—of any group in the United States. They are also making rapid strides, in the face of extreme prejudice, to improve their situation.

Facts have not prevented the stereotype from being held, however. Hispanics have encountered prejudice all over the United States in varying degrees. As with other minorities, each Spanish-speaking group has met the strongest resistance where its numbers have been highest. Mexicans, for example, have had the most difficult time in the Southwest and California, while Puerto Ricans have found trouble in New York. And the prejudice has been largely based on skin color—the darker the color, the stronger the hatred.

Mexican Americans—
Settlers of the Southwest

Ironically, the Mexican Americans who first encountered prejudice in the Southwest were not latecomers; they were descendants of the region's first European settlers. In 1598 the Spanish explorer Don Juan de Oñate led a band of four hundred men, women, and children across the Rio Grande into a territory he called New Mexico. (Today this region is made up of the states of Texas, California, New Mexico, and Arizona as well as parts of Colorado, Utah, and Nevada.) Descendants of this group and other Spanish-speaking settlers farmed and ranched in the area undisturbed for well over two hundred years.

Anti-Mexican feelings in the United States were fueled by border disputes and by incidents such as the siege of the Alamo, in which Americans were killed defending a fort in Texas, which had declared itself independent from Mexico. These disputes led to the Mexican War, fought from 1846 to 1848, and wartime patriotic feeling in the United States further hardened anti-Mexican attitudes. At the end of the war, a defeated Mexico signed the vast region over to the United States in the Treaty of Guadalupe Hidalgo. The treaty guaranteed the people of the former Mexican territory United States citizenship, property rights, and religious freedom. But the Mexicans were soon overwhelmed by advancing tides of English-speaking settlers, who arrived in California during the gold rush of the 1850s and elsewhere in the Southwest after the building of the transcontinental railway in the 1870s. The Mexicans became a barely tolerated minority, and one by one they lost their rights. Through threats, legal trickery, and outright theft, they also lost their land.

Thus the Mexicans largely retreated to small mountain villages, where they lived in poverty and held on to their traditional language and customs. They might have remained a small and nearly forgotten minority, were it not for events of the early 1900s. From 1900 to about 1920, Mexico was torn by social and political strife. Hundreds of thousands of its people fled north, crossing the border legally or illegally to search for a better life in the United States. By this time agriculture in the Southwest had expanded to the point where large numbers of ranch hands and field workers were required. The railroads were also expanding and needed unskilled laborers to lay tracks.

The Mexicans, like the Asian immigrants, often found work as low-paid contract laborers, moving from job to job. Some returned to Mexico during slow periods when work was hard to find and then recrossed the border when jobs were available again. Eventually many settled in United States cities, especially Los Angeles, where they lived in slum areas called *barrios*. And from California and the Southwest, the Mexicans fanned out into the Midwest and other areas of the country, taking jobs in factories, construction, and other fields.

This vast influx led to a rising tide of anti-Mexican feeling, and the stereotype of the dirty, lazy, irresponsible Mexican began to arise. The effects of the prejudice were devastating for the immigrants. Contractors often thought nothing of cheating them out of their wages. Violence broke out in Texas and other areas of the West and Southwest, where "Anglos" (English-speaking people) feared the immigrants would undermine society. One of the hottest points of controversy was education. Many Anglos felt that Mexican children .should be separated from white children or perhaps not be educated at all. As one farmer put it, "Mexicans . . .

don't want responsibility, they want just to float along, sing songs, smoke cigarettes. Education doesn't make them any happier. . . . It only makes them dissatisfied."

The Mexicans, meanwhile, were slow to adopt American ways for several reasons. Their homeland was nearby, and most kept in contact with relatives there. Many crossed and recrossed the border continually, and there was also a steady stream of new Mexican immigrants arriving. All of these things made it easy for the Mexicans to maintain their traditional language and customs. But these differences only fueled the prejudice they encountered.

By the late 1920s growing feeling against the Mexicans led some people to press for restrictions on immigration. Illegal entry became a criminal offense, and a border patrol was established to check the flow of "wetbacks" (so named because they waded across the Rio Grande). But Congress did not limit or halt legal Mexican immigration—not through lack of prejudice, but because farmers testified to their need for cheap labor and managed to block the move. Many farmers said they preferred Mexican labor. According to one, "A nigger is unappreciative. [A Mexican] is just like a dog; slap him and he'll lick your hand." Said another, "I do not want to see the condition arise again when white men who are reared and educated in our schools have got to bend their backs and skin their fingers" doing field work.

When the Great Depression of the 1930s began, Mexicans were at the bottom of society in terms of jobs and income. As jobs became scarcer and scarcer, competition became fiercer—and it was usually the Mexicans who lost out. Employers adopted new policies, hiring only white workers. Thus many Mexicans were forced to go on welfare. And to cut its welfare costs and reduce the number of surplus workers, the United States government began an exportation program, shipping Mexican workers indiscriminately back to their home villages. But the returnees found things no better there— Mexico also suffered a depression.

Those Mexican Americans who remained in the United States continued to be treated as foreigners, even though they were permanent residents and in many cases had been born in the country. World War II brought increased economic opportunities, and Mexican Americans also fought bravely in the United States armed forces. These developments were overshadowed, however, by a series of events that reflected the depth of prejudice against Mexicans.

The first was the Sleepy Lagoon incident of 1942, in which a Mexican youth was beaten to death by unknown assailants in Los Angeles. A group of Mexicans was arrested for the crime, and at the group's trial the prosecution leaned heavily on the idea that Mexicans generally had an uncontrollable desire to kill, stemming from their Aztec Indian blood. The argument convinced the jury, and the Mexicans were convicted on circumstantial evidence. Their conviction was later overturned, but the following year riots broke out between bands of Mexican-American youths and Anglos. Called the "zoot-suit riots" (for the somewhat outlandish suits the Mexicans wore), these incidents whipped up anti-Mexican feeling.

As the economy picked up during and after World War II, Mexicans once again began to pour into the United States. Some entered illegally, and some came as contract workers—*braceros*—under an agreement worked out by the United States and Mexican governments in 1942. The illegal immigrants and the *braceros*

*Zoot-suiters accused of the murder of a Mexican youth
in Los Angeles in 1942 on their way to court.
The prosecution's case was sketchy but racist arguments
led to a conviction. Although the verdict was later
overturned, anti-Mexican feelings remained high.*

*Cesar Chavez (center) led the labor movement in the
1960s that fought for fair wages and better
working conditions for Mexican-American migrant workers.*

were often willing to work for half the going rate or less, and this undercut the wages of other Mexican Americans.

Underpaid and surrounded by prejudice and antipathy, the Mexican Americans began to organize labor unions and social-action groups. When the *bracero* program ended in the 1960s, they began to demand the pay white workers would receive. The result was strikes, such as the Delano, California, grape-pickers' strike in 1965 that was led by labor leader Cesar Chavez. Riding the waves of the civil rights movement of the 1960s, other Mexican Americans began to press claims for lost land and to seek an end to discrimination. Their struggle became known as the Chicano movement (the name "Chicano" is thought to have come from the Spanish word *mejicano*, meaning Mexican.)

These civil rights efforts met with mixed success. The more than eight million Mexican Americans in the United States today continue to face enormous problems. They earn less and on the whole have fewer years of education than the general population. But more and more opportunities are open to them in education and employment. And it is difficult to compare statistics on their income with statistics for the total population of the United States because as a group, the Mexicans are younger (and would therefore be expected to earn less) than the population as a whole. About half of the Mexican Americans are also first- or second-generation immigrants, struggling to get established, and illegal immigration continues to be a problem.

The Puerto Ricans
Like the Philippines, Puerto Rico became a territory of the United States in 1898, at the end of the Spanish-American War. After 1917 the people of Puerto Rico

became United States citizens at birth. But the nearly four centuries of Spanish rule that had preceded these events ensured that the Puerto Ricans' language and customs would remain largely Hispanic. Thus, from the start, Puerto Ricans were different from English-speaking Americans. And their mixed racial background—European, African, and Indian—made them easy targets for the prejudices of the white majority.

Small numbers of Puerto Ricans moved to the mainland of the United States throughout the early 1900s. Usually they traveled by ship to New York City, the East Coast's major port. But large-scale migration did not begin until the 1940s, when regularly scheduled low-cost passenger flights to and from the island were started. Most of the Puerto Ricans who traveled to the mainland then took cheap night-coach flights to New York, where they could join relatives and friends who had already made the trip. By 1970 there were 1.5 million Puerto Ricans in the United States, and more in New York City than in the island's capital, San Juan.

The Puerto Ricans' reasons for leaving the island were chiefly economic—Puerto Rico's standard of living improved dramatically in the early years of the century, but it still lagged far behind the standards on the mainland. Many of the Puerto Ricans who migrated were poor farmers. In New York and other cities, they found a life far different from the simple rural life they had known on their sunny island. Legally classed as whites, they soon learned that it was impossible for

*Children playing in
a rubble-strewn lot in
New York's Spanish
Harlem slum area*

them to find housing in white neighborhoods. Puerto Rican ghettos, such as New York's Spanish Harlem, developed near the black ghettos that already existed. Only low-paying, low-prestige jobs were open to the Puerto Ricans, in factories, hotels and restaurants, and the like. Their wages were scarcely enough to pay the rent or buy the warm clothes they needed for the cold winters of the North. In one notorious 1940s case, sixty Puerto Ricans working at a Chicago foundry were housed in unheated railway cars by their employer, who then deducted room and board from their pay.

To a degree, all the immigrant groups that have entered the United States—Irish, Italians, and so on—have suffered some similar problems. But in most cases these groups have overcome their immigrant status within a generation or two. In the case of the Puerto Ricans, however, racial prejudice acted to keep them at the bottom of society.

The extent to which skin color was a factor in the Puerto Ricans' poverty is brought out clearly in Piri Thomas's autobiographical book *Down These Mean Streets*. Thomas grew up in Harlem during the 1940s, and in one chapter he describes how he and a friend went together to apply for jobs selling housewares. Both were Puerto Rican; both had identical backgrounds and qualifications. The only difference between them was that while Thomas was dark-skinned, his friend was light-skinned. And the friend, not Thomas, was hired.

Citizens treated like foreigners, the Puerto Ricans, like the Mexicans, tended to hold onto their Spanish language and culture. They were in constant contact with relatives on the island, and many traveled back and forth frequently. A high percentage of Puerto Rican children dropped out of school, both from economic necessity and because of difficulties with language and the Anglo orientation of the material presented in school. Lack of education thus became another handicap for the Puerto Ricans in their attempt to break through the barriers of prejudice.

Throughout the 1960s and 1970s, Puerto Ricans remained at the bottom of the economic ladder, in most cities earning less even than blacks. And their poverty contributed to high rates of crime and dependence on welfare. Recently, however, the picture has begun to change. Bilingual education programs are helping more Puerto Rican children finish school, and more Puerto Ricans are entering the middle class. Most of the approximately two million Puerto Ricans now living on the mainland still work for low wages as unskilled or semi-skilled workers. But like the Mexicans, the Puerto Ricans are a young group—their average age was under twenty in the early 1970s. As they gain experience, it is likely that they will continue to advance.

The Cubans and Other Hispanics

The Cubans who have immigrated to the United States have done so under circumstances that are distinctly different from those of most other Hispanic immigrants. The vast majority of the Cuban immigrants fled the Marxist regime of Cuban president Fidel Castro, who took power in the 1950s. The greatest numbers of Cubans arrived from 1965 to 1973, when the Freedom Airlift was operated to take them to the United States. Another large group arrived in small boats in 1980, when Castro briefly relaxed emigration restrictions. As political refugees, the Cubans were helped by public and private welfare agencies to relocate and find jobs.

At first most of the refugees clustered in Miami, Florida, in the hope that Castro would be overthrown and they would be able to return. As this hope dimmed, many moved on to settle in other parts of the country. But more than half of the one million Cuban Americans in the United States still live in or near Miami. There the massive Cuban influx has stirred racial tension between whites and Hispanics and also between Hispanics and blacks, who see in the newcomers competition for jobs and housing.

But while most other Hispanic immigrants have been poor people seeking a better way of life, the Cubans represented a cross section of society. They included the wealthy as well as the poor, and many were highly educated and skilled. This has enabled them to achieve a standard of living that is markedly higher than that of other Hispanic Americans. However, the fact that some of the 1980 refugees were convicted criminals damaged the Cubans' image, even though the criminals were a small minority.

Some three million other Hispanics live in the United States. They trace their roots to nearly every country of Central and South America. Some, like the Cubans, have fled political repression; others, like the Mexicans and Puerto Ricans, have come seeking a better life.

English-speaking Americans often tend to lump these groups together, assuming, for example, that any Hispanic is a Puerto Rican or a Mexican. Thus the other nationalities have fallen heir to the prejudices that already existed toward the earlier arrivals. But the civil rights movement of the 1960s affected Hispanics as well as other minorities, and the different Hispanic groups have started to work together to improve their lot. One critical step was the passage of the Bilingual Education Act of 1968, which makes funds available for education in children's native languages as well as in English. Open-admissions policies at many colleges are allow-

A Cuban refugee, one of the thousands Castro allowed to leave Cuba in 1980, kisses the ground upon arriving in Key West, Florida. Despite a political welcome, heightened racial tensions between Hispanics and whites as well as between Hispanics and blacks have resulted from such massive influxes of immigrants.

ing more Hispanics to continue their education. As with blacks, however, these steps have sometimes provoked a backlash of racial feeling.

Still, much prejudice remains. The frustration felt by many Hispanic Americans is perhaps best summed up in the words of Eduardo Perez, a community leader in the *barrio* of Los Angeles. Perez is quoted by the author Stan Steiner in his study of the Mexican Americans, *La Raza:* "I wish God had made people blind. Then a touch of the hand, a word of the mouth, would be all they would need to know their neighbor. People now judge each other by how they look, not by how they are. . . . Our eyes betray us."

8 | A Denial of Humanity

Racial prejudice is far from being unique to white Americans. We have seen how ethnocentrism colored the myths of the Chinese and the American Indians. And prejudice has often led to conflict between minority groups in the United States. Some blacks, for example, hold deep prejudices against Jews and other groups. But white racial prejudice was a feature of American life before the founding of the United States, and it has remained so, to one degree or another, ever since.

The prejudicial stereotypes that white Americans have held about various other racial groups have had nothing to do with reality. Nearly every nonwhite group in the United States has at some point been criticized for being lazy, filthy, ignorant, irresponsible, and, by nature, untrustworthy. In fact, the similarities among the stereotypes of blacks, Indians, Asians, and Hispanics are striking clues to the falseness of the pictures—if it were true that groups, rather than individuals, could display such traits, why would all nonwhites, and only nonwhites, have them?

Many white Americans have been far too ready to believe that any nonwhite group is inferior. Some psychologists have suggested that such feelings stem not from observation of other groups but from deep feelings of inadequacy on the part of prejudiced people. People who hold deep prejudices against others may see traits in themselves—laziness or dishonesty, for example—that they cannot accept. So, in their minds, they assign these traits to other people, people who look as different as possible from themselves.

Social attitudes about racial differences have changed dramatically in recent years. Discriminatory laws have been stricken down and replaced with laws that attempt to guarantee equal treatment for all. But ending legalized discrimination is not the same as ending prejudice, and prejudice lingers on. Recent years have seen it take new forms—whites taking flight to expensive suburbs, for example, as blacks and other racial groups begin to move up from slum housing in the cities. Social Darwinism lingers in disputes over such measures as IQ scores: When nonwhites score lower than whites on these tests, some whites claim the results reflect natural inferiority, while others say they reflect the nonwhites' disadvantaged position.

The debate over the influence of heredity and environment on intelligence may never be fully settled. It is a fact that some people, in every race, are more intelligent than others. It is also a fact that as each ethnic group in the United States has improved its position economically, its IQ test scores have risen—indicating that social advantages play an important role in the scores. People at the bottom of the social ladder must contend with poverty, malnutrition, and disease. Daily life is a struggle for existence, and there is little time left for education. When prejudice and discrimination act to thwart any hope of moving up, it is likely that such people may give up their aspirations altogether.

This is a tragic loss—not only for the people who have given up, but for society as a whole. Everyone in society is interconnected; whether we like it or not, we all pull together to move the society in whatever direction it is taking. When someone is deprived of the opportunity to contribute his or her full potential, we are all losers. Perhaps the Mexican child who left school early to work in the fields could have been a surgeon.

Perhaps a young black who cannot afford a college education has the makings of a statesman, a peacemaker who could solve the international deadlock over nuclear arms. At the very least, prejudice impoverishes human lives by preventing people from getting to know others—people who might have been rare and wonderful friends.

Prejudice is doubly tragic in a democracy like the United States, which was founded on the principle of equality. In the early 1960s, as the civil rights movement began to expose the extent of racism to the eyes of the world, United States Secretary of State Dean Rusk wrote:

The principles of racial equality and nondiscrimination are imperatives of the American society with its many racial strains. In the degree to which we ourselves practice these principles our voice will carry conviction. . . . American actions which fall short of Constitutional standards safeguarding individual freedom and dignity prejudice our position before the world.

The greater awareness created by the civil rights movement has helped lessen discrimination, but it has not been enough to end prejudice. That will require more effort—and more time. Each of us needs to learn as much as he or she can about other racial groups, to understand their cultural differences and different points of view. We need to train ourselves to think logically, not emotionally, about other people, so that we can pick out the irrationalities of racial stereotypes. And above all, we must get to know individuals of other races, so that we can learn firsthand that people of all colors are, after all, just people.

Ending prejudice will require an enormous effort in schools, homes, and businesses on the part of every person in the country. But if the United States is to be the nation that its founders dreamed of, the effort must be made. As the scholar Ashley Montagu wrote, "Every American, as an American, must make himself responsible for the elimination of racism, for racism is inhuman, ethically wrong, constitutionally intolerable, and a denial of humanity."

For Further Reading

Among the many books dealing with the general subject of racial prejudice in the United States, two standouts are Ashley Montagu's *Man's Most Dangerous Myth: The Fallacy of Race* (1975), and Bruno Bettelheim and Morris Janowitz's sociological study *Social Change and Prejudice* (1964). Thomas Sowell's *Ethnic America: A History* (1981) gives a historical overview of the experiences of several racial and ethnic groups. Other useful books include Ronald T. Takaki's *Iron Cages: Race and Culture in 19th-Century America* (1979); Thomas F. Gossett's *Race: The History of an Idea in America* (1963); Roger Daniels and Harry H. L. Kitani's *American Racism: Exploration of the Nature of Prejudice* (1970); and Charles Y. Glock and Ellen Seigelman, editors of *Prejudice USA* (1969).

Scores of books deal specifically with the problems faced by blacks. George M. Frederickson's *The Black Image in the White Mind* (1971) gives a devastating picture of the early years, as does Winthrop D. Jordan's *The White Man's Burden: Historical Origins of Racism in the United States* (1974). Another important book is John Hope Franklin's *Racial Equality in America* (1976).

Notable among books on prejudice against American Indians is Robert F. Burkholder, Jr.'s *The White Man's Indian: Images of the American Indian from Columbus to the Present* (1978). Vine Deloria, Jr., gives an account of recent problems in *The Indian Affair* (1974). Essays on Asian Americans are collected by Norris Hindley, Jr., in *The Asian American: The Historical Experience* (1976). Other books on Asians include Stuart Creighton Miller's *The Unwelcome Immigrant: The American Image of the Chinese,*

1785–1882 (1969); Betty Lee Sung's *Mountain of Gold: The Story of the Chinese in America* (1967); and Robert A. Wilson and Bill Hosokawa's *East to America: A History of the Japanese in America* (1980). The problems faced by Hispanics are brought out in two collections of essays, *Readings on La Raza* (1974), edited by Matt S. Meier and Feliciano Rivera, and *The Puerto Ricans* (1973), edited by Kal Wagenheim with Olga Jimenez de Wagenheim. Stan Steiner's *La Raza: The Mexican Americans* (1969) is a colorful account of the Chicano movement.

Index